THE GOSPEL ACCORDING TO TONY
SOPRANO

THE GOSPEL ACCORDING TO TONY

SOPRANO

An *Unauthorized* Look Into the Soul of
TV's Top Mob Boss and His Family

BY CHRIS SEAY

Jeremy P. Tarcher/Putnam
a member of
Penguin Putnam Inc.
New York

Most Tarcher/Putnam books are available at special quantity discounts for bulk purchase for sales promotions, premiums, fund-raising, and educational needs. Special books or book excerpts also can be created to fit specific needs. For details, write Putnam Special Markets, 375 Hudson Street, New York, NY 10014.

Jeremy P. Tarcher/Putnam
a member of
Penguin Putnam Inc.
375 Hudson Street
New York, NY 10014
www.penguinputnam.com

An application to register this book for cataloguing has been submitted to the Library of Congress

ISBN 1-58542-194-4

Printed in the United States of America
10 9 8 7 6 5 4 3 2 1

This book is printed on acid-free paper. ∞

Book design by Relevant Solutions
Bobby Jones, Daniel Ariza, Greg Lutze
www.relevant-solutions.com

RELEVANT BOOKS
a division of
Relevant Media Group Inc.
P.O. Box 951127
Lake Mary, FL 32795
www.relevant-books.com

Relevant Books is a registered trademark of Relevant Media Group, Inc., and is registered in the U.S. Patent and Trademark Office.

In Memory of
Oliver Ted Stanford
A man who knew well the pain and sorrow of life, and the
utter joy of redemption.

I'm going flying, I wish y'all could see me. I just passed a
yellow moon, and the stars are glad to see me. I got me a
window seat on a Cadillac for glory. Mother Mary's kissin'
me, she's gonna tell me a bedtime story.

ACKNOWLEDGEMENTS

To my beautiful wife and loving girls: your patience and love mean the world to me. Ecclesia and especially the staff (Chad, Christy, Tim, Jamie, Steve, Craig, Tyndall, Laci, and Robbie), thank you for the help and commitment to our shared mission. Brandi Wheeler and family, your hospitality has made this book possible; thank you for sharing with me one of the most peaceful places I have ever known. Stephen Ratcliff, your help has been tremendous. My brothers, Brian and Robbie, who share my journey in so many ways, I value your support. To Joel and Denise at Penguin for believing in this book and making it happen at breakneck speed. The team at Relevant, you do great work, and especially Cara Baker, my editor, who has worked endless hours and understands my style and humor—thank you.

There are many people who have loved me and made contributions to this book through our relationship: The Emergent Senior Fellows (www.emergentvillage.org), my family (Mom, Dad, Jennifer, and Jessica), Greg Garrett, Acts 29 Network, UBA, Damah Film Festival (www.damah.com), Leadership Network and Brad Smith, Mark Oestreicher, and Youth Specialties.

To Justin Hyde, my co-author and beloved friend, you have worked with me tirelessly on this project and it would have been painful if I had done it without you. Here is to better days!

CONTENTS

INTRODUCTION

At first, my wife was troubled by my love of *The Sopranos*. An educated person with a spiritual calling should not consume such a large weekly dose of obscenity and violence. For God's sake, what kind of husband helps put the kids down to sleep and then flips on HBO to watch Tony and Big Pussy shoot the Bevalaqua kid full of lead?

I remember one night watching Tony in the Bada Bing cursing up a blue streak as a throng of naked women with near perfect bodies crowded around him. I was desperately hoping my wife would not walk in the room. I'd be caught, embarrassed like a kid on a burnt sofa cushion with a handful of matches. I considered turning it off. I flipped over to CNN a few times, but always turned back.

Despite my desire to find a higher moral ground, I continued to race home every Sunday night after church to be with the Soprano family. In time, I decided to not only watch the show, but to speak openly about my affection-turned-obsession with this HBO series. The tension never leaves me, and it shouldn't. There are still some episodes, however, that I would not re-watch to this day. The scene where Dr. Mclfi is raped in a parking garage is the worst thing I have ever witnessed on television or the big screen. When it was over I just felt sick, like I had been kicked in the stomach. So I understood my wife's concern. She just couldn't imagine how violence + sex + greed = beauty. She hypothesized two major theories to explain my newfound love of *The Sopranos*.

1. The profanity in excess is amusing. Maybe I enjoy hearing "fuck" used so many different ways. The word becomes almost poetic in its ability to illustrate everything from great pasta to the Federal Bureau of Investigation.

2. Tony Soprano represents the alpha male, and I secretly wish to become more like him. He is likeable, successful, and powerful—life and death often hinge on his words.

While both of these hypotheses may harbor some truth, they only begin to scratch the surface. With a story that seems totally contrary to my life experience, *The Sopranos'* creator, David Chase, has tapped into a part of me I have managed to keep hidden even from myself.

In time this story, and my introspective response to it, beckoned my spouse as well. We were soon watching Tony and Carmela together, side by side on the couch. She walked out of the room when Tony killed his best friend Pussy, but like me, she kept coming back for more.

St. Augustine speaks of the story of Scripture as a "pharmacon," the Latin word from which we derive "pharmacy." It literally means poison and remedy. Like most medicine, it has the power to heal and to kill. If it is misinterpreted or used to support one's own views it can destroy, but used as a source of wisdom, it offers life to those who approach it humbly. In the same way, *The Sopranos* serves as a prescription for the soul. It has the power to condemn or restore. It is much more complex than a mere mob tale or your typical mini-series about a suburban family. It is about life and death. To misread *The Sopranos* as a glorification of violence or a cheap comedy about middle-class America is to not read it at all. Like all art, it must be interpreted.

The closest thing that I know to this type of personal awakening via television is the love my family has with *M.A.S.H.* Some of my greatest memories growing up are of sitting on the floor with my parents and siblings eating popcorn as we watched Hawkeye, B.J., and Colonels Blake and Potter. We spent time with them almost every night, and they became part of our family. Dad taped every episode on our old Betamax VCR. It wasn't until my late teens, however, that I realized there were hidden reasons why we were drawn to the dark villages of South Korea each night. My Dad's dad, Earl Martin Seay, was killed in the Korean War just before my father turned eight weeks old. When we watched *M.A.S.H.* it was as if my grandfather sat there with us for thirty minutes. I never knew him, rarely spoke of him, but desperately missed him. And although we tried to conceal it, we thought of him with every jab at the futility of war, the endless crude jokes, the mention of family back home, and always with each man who died. *M.A.S.H.* did not air for seventeen seasons because of its superb acting and poignant writing. It captured America's heart for reasons much more meaningful. And so it is with *The Sopranos*.

The Sopranos steps to center stage and forces me to respond. It provokes me, excites me, pisses me off, and pries back the exterior to peek into the darkest parts of my soul. The show actually sees me as I am. It pokes at my spirit with unsavory stories. And the stories it tells are pathetic. The characters take selfishness to a new level, selfishness that does not stop with subtle lies, lavish spending on momentary comforts, and a preoccupation with the admiration of others. It sinks to murder, theft, torture, extortion, adultery, and worse. I want to be sanctimonious and push these hideous characters away. But I cannot. We're just too much alike.

I can't really say that I enjoy television. CNN can be helpful. CNBC is depressing. The networks are predictable. And MTV has become an atrocity. But the first time I watched *The Sopranos* my heart raced. It was more than a TV show. It was an experience. The story grabbed me and I became a part of it, or it became a part of me. And I know I'm not alone. This book explores the many reasons why *The Sopranos* has connected deeply with American culture and exposes the mysteries about faith and life that emerge just behind the curtains of baked ziti and Armani suits.

So let this book serve as a contemplative guide to a story set in New Jersey that truly has the power to heal or to kill. And as it is said, "He who has ears to hear, let him hear."[1]

CULTURAL REFLECTION
WHY *THE SOPRANOS* STRIKES A CHORD

The Sopranos has held the imagination of the world at gunpoint. This story of an upper-middle class suburban family has found an unprecedented place in the heart of cable television subscribers. This fictional family slips in under the radar and subverts viewers who would typically not take part in violence, crime, and deceit in any other context. Yet, every Sunday night, while sitting safely in their living room, millions of people become a third party to criminal activity.

The show's "richly textured comic realism and truthfulness" and Sinatra-esque mystique forces its ever-increasing global audience to keep coming back for more—whether they like it or not.[1] It awakens something deep within its viewers and is recognized by its critics as "the best television drama ever!"[2] Is this highly regarded HBO mini-series merely feeding off the culture's morbid fascination with the mafia? Or have Tony and the family tapped into something much greater than *The Godfather*?

This story calls attention to something missing from our

lives, a chasm left empty by a lack of faith, a deep desire to belong, and shallow capitalistic values. But the show does not fill the void. It exposes it. It paints a picture of a journey we all travel to find purpose and meaning in an otherwise meaningless life. Viewers see their lives more clearly as a result and cannot ignore the mixture of created beauty and vile impulses. Despite the immense beauty of humanity, which is created "imago dei," in the image of God, the fallen self contains darkness and depravity. French thinker, mathematician, and scientist Blaise Pascal said, "Man's greatness comes from knowing he is wretched: a tree does not know it is wretched. Thus it is wretched to know that one is wretched, but there is greatness in knowing one is wretched."[3] Pascal was correct, and *The Sopranos* has the power to lead you to greatness as it amplifies the wretchedness in us all.

More than eleven million households tuned in to the highly anticipated final episode of the third season. As Uncle Junior sang a striking Italian aria, the families came together amidst food, wine, and song. The moment conjured up feelings of intimacy and joy that seemed like memories of Christmas as a child. Everyone was together. Everything was right. The hate and distrust that plague the story line seemed to vanish, and people everywhere learned forgiveness. When the hot-tempered father with his arm around his son listened solemnly to the uncle who tried to have him killed, the pride in our own families was quietly exposed. Fathers, mothers, daughters, and sons across the world remain separated by petty sins, yet this criminal family is modeling for us a story of forgiveness.

Food, wine, and music are only temporary diversions from the conflict and danger around the corner for Tony Soprano. A potential betrayer, an angry grief-stricken daughter, and a Russian warrior with a lethal plan were still potential threats to Tony as the third season ended. Many fans violently threw objects at their screens in disbelief that the storyline would hit pause for more than a year with these major conflicts unresolved.

But in every episode of every season, Chase focused on the heart of his story, the place that truly draws us in, the family. HBO calls it family re-defined, but it always looks a lot like home. *The Sopranos* has connected with an American audience in a way that the Cosbys never could, and for many, this connection has turned obsession.

Ann Zivotsky writes, "I think I'm obsessed with *The Sopranos*. I wonder if Dr. Melfi can fit me in for a session?"[4] It should be assumed that Ann Zivotsky is a very competent woman, an excellent journalist, and an active participant in a typical social life in Orange County (which would not be typical anywhere else), and she can't get enough. It seems no one can.

These are not crazy people. *Sopranos* fans are not lunatics or violent. They are not at all like *Star Trek* fans. This obsession takes on a very different behavior. You don't see Joe the accountant flying off to a *Sopranos* convention or showing up at the office in an Italian suit with his shirt open to expose his gaudy jewelry and chest hair. This show does not command imitation; it requires contemplation. One naturally begins to examine his life, family relationships, finances, and the God who created man in this miserable state. This contemplation raises questions much deeper than the sociology and economics of mob life. It probes the deeper mysteries of life: the problem of evil, the existence of God, how we experience the divine, the nature of heaven and hell, and the consequences of our actions.

Hannah Brown phrases the question this way in a column for *The Jerusalem Post*, "Why are so many people crazy about *The Sopranos*? How is it that Israelis, who have enough real violence to deal with, are drawn to this story of a man who chooses and is comfortable with a violent lifestyle?"[5]

The simple, honest answer is that Tony's a likable guy. He shoots people in a way that forces us to admit, "Well, I guess he had to do it." He cheats on his wife and you think of it as a vocational hazard. The guy worries about everything and it seems to exonerate his guilt. If you're going to kill people, steal, and commit adultery, at least you feel bad about it. He's not a sociopath after all. Tony and the family are very much like the rest of humankind—worrying and feeling guilt as a result of their actions. Tony could be your boss. Your son. Your husband. Your father. Even you. And this explains why *The Sopranos* is so dangerously addictive and so disturbing. Stephen Holden writes, "Tony's brutality is all the more disturbing because it erupts from within a social framework of apparent normalcy."[6]

The Sopranos shines light into dark areas. It calls hidden secrets to the surface and creates a heightened awareness of the flawed state of mankind. It happens unexpectedly, like spotting the overlooked grime lingering under your finger-nails. At once you see your hands as they are, filthy and dis-gusting, and you are appalled. Similarly, you watch the show and you may find yourself wanting Tony to kill the traitor, deceive the FBI, and exact sadistic revenge on the worst kinds of people. Your response may be unprecedented and even shocking to you. But you know that something the characters did or said struck deep into the heart of who you are. For ten bucks a month, HBO gives you a new self-awareness. We watch Tony, Carmela, and the rest of the crew, and we see ourselves. It is more than just sixty minutes of action, music, and dialogue. It is a lens that has shaped the way we view the world. Reality steps in and paints an accurate picture as it destroys the illusion of suburban bliss and exposes the vanity, greed, and hypocrisy that typify this culture.

When Silvio gets sick and throws up before he has to kill his best friend, Pussy, it doesn't have to be explained. The view-ers' stomachs are churning as well. When Tony, the chronic adulterer, tells Carmela, "You're not just in my life, you are my life," fans of the show put faith in the unfaithful Mafioso and believe. Because we see ourselves in him, we want to believe that Tony is actually good, and that consequently we are good.

The world loves this adulterous, lying, murderous thief because he is real, raw, and exposed. Caryn James, another commentator for *The New York Times*, wrote, "Emphatically middle class, [Tony] is like one of your neighbors, but with a more dangerous job."[7]

But there is something about Tony Soprano that is too real for us—too close to everyday life. As Peter Kreeft says, "To look at a man with both eyes open is terrifying and wonderful, like a roller-coaster ride. It yields a great sense of depth, a third dimension, just as two physical eyes do."[8] We watch Tony and we see ourselves, and that scares us.

Our culture has become so good at covering up the dark—covering up the real—that we are taken aback by such penetrating pictures of reality. Selfish motives rise to the surface and call all of our actions into question. We are driven by our own lust instead of the greater good, and it is to our shame. We are mortified by our lack of moral integrity. We rely on the false so much that when the true story of our sin is revealed, we are forced into the arms of therapy and medication. Still, honest people crave this reality, this acknowledgement in the self-centeredness of humankind. But what we desire most—spiritual realization—we also fear most. This journey will be painful. But we search for truth nonetheless, because we hope for something better.

How can one become a better person watching a series that is violent and sexually deviant, portrays criminal behavior, and disrespects the sacred vows that bind the family? Many will say it's not possible. They will likely mock the aim of this book and especially the intentions of *Sopranos* creator David Chase, who is seen as cashing in on extreme violence and sexuality. In fact, if you often agree with Christian conservative Pat Robertson, then this is not the book for you. It would be a good idea to put this book down now and turn away slowly. But if you have even a small understanding of what motivates Ann Zivotsky's obsession and openness to spiritual insight, then you've come to the right place.

Pundits claim violence begets more violence. The belief is that the brain is a sponge which simply absorbs what it sees and hears and mimics it. They say, "Garbage in—garbage out," "What I see, I will become," and so forth. This philosophy may sound reasonable to many, but it is deeply flawed. It is merely a tool used by religions to control followers. It teaches people they should avoid art, literature, film, and discourse which do not fit into the religious organization's worldview. It's an extremist view that allows no room for moderation. It's like taking the adage, "You are what you eat," literally. But if all you eat is Velveeta cheese you will not become Velveeta cheese, although you will likely get sick. In the same way, watching violent television will not make you violent. However, it should be understood that your mind should feast on more than your weekly dose of James Gandolfini and Jamie-Lynn Sigler. But based on the fact you are currently reading this book, you already know your way to the bookstore and will likely read something else when finished with this.

Art should reflect reality, not religious fantasy. Turning the scandalous men of the Bible like Abraham, Solomon, and Moses into Mr. Rogers-type figures robs the biblical narrative of its power. These men were deeply flawed, not unlike

Tony Soprano. Abraham pimps out the matriarch of the Judeo-Christian faith to powerful kings, and his nephew Lot offers his virgin daughter to the townspeople to be gang-raped. Solomon takes a new wife almost daily, and Moses murders a man in a fit of rage. When everyone is near perfect there is no progress. No direction. No redemption. Nothing real people can relate to. It is only when a mirror is held up to reflect our own imperfection that we begin to comprehend our need for change. These flawed men and women are broken in the same ways you and I are, and therefore have something to say to us.

Steven Isaac, in a review for *Focus on the Family* magazine, points to the depravity of *The Sopranos*, saying, "Tony deals drugs, oversees a gambling operation and is a master of extortion. Henchmen carry out hits in gruesome fashion. One opponent's head gets blown off. A man's back snaps when he's repeatedly rammed with a car. And baseball bat-wielding hoodlums attack a group of black protesters who just happen to picket the 'wrong' company." *The Sopranos* uses "fuck" an average of about once a minute, Isaac estimates. When using the word "shit" or other vulgarities and racial slurs, the average doubles or even triples. The show features nude dancers and graphic scenes of sexuality and prostitution. Isaac continues, "*The Sopranos* is a repulsive peep show that celebrates the behavior of self-destructive people who live devoid of conscience and bereft of morality or human decency."

It may not seem we are that corrupt, but these mobsters only take our same vices to the extreme. In the portrayal of this excess, wrapped in a veneer of apparent normalcy, we truly recognize our own depravity.

The book of Proverbs says wisdom exposes the foolishness of our ways. In the same understanding, *The Sopranos* and David Chase are truly wise. The show has the ability to expose follies, air dirty laundry, and alter our current path. The task of this book is to guide the reflection that happens naturally to everyone who participates in this story, for it is in this reflection that we become better people.

THE MAN BEHIND THE MOB

David Chase, the mastermind behind this television phenomenon, must have his fingers on the pulse of the American psyche. His show sheds light on American life and exposes the violence, perversion, and greed that permeate our current cultural landscape. Chase brilliantly displays the middle-class family as it struggles with the issues of right and wrong within a morally relativistic society.

Chase discovered his love of all things creative through music and the local fame of a New Jersey garage band. He says, "Music was really my doorway into the arts."[9] HBO has allowed this television icon to find his voice, and millions of people have made his stories a part of their own. But as an artist, Chase has been frustrated. He views his career in television as a sign of weakness, a failure to pursue his dreams in film. He says regretfully, "I took the money. I didn't have the guts to stop it ... I compromised. Hugely."[10] Making money doesn't satisfy him; it is never enough.

Born in Mt. Vernon, New York, this bi-coastal writer/director grew up in Caldwell, New Jersey, the hometown of Tony Soprano. Chase was raised by his parents in a Baptist church and later followed his roots to a Baptist school, Wake Forest University. Although his parents met at a church youth group meeting and insisted that he attend Sunday school and church as a child, Chase claims the church thing "never quite took."[11] But the themes Chase pens in *The Sopranos* are full of the drama of the biblical narratives and possess an invariable search for spiritual truth.

Chase describes Tony and his peers' actions honestly, "We know he does bad things. But he's effective at what he does in his context; in his world he's good at it ... that's what he's chosen. He made a choice a long time ago to do this. And my conception of the series has always been that it's a show about a bunch of people, starting with him, who have made a deal with the devil. Everybody in the show, to a certain extent, has made a, to a greater or lesser degree, except for the kids, I guess, have made a deal with the devil."[12]

Chase not only brings his religious upbringing to the story, but his family life as well. The only character more compelling than Tony Soprano in this series is Tony's mom, Livia, who is loosely based on Chase's own mother. Livia is the controlling mother who holds all the cards and paints herself as the eternal victim. Chase's own wife was astounded when Nancy Merchand brought Livia Soprano's character to life. The similarity was beyond belief; it was like his mother, Norma De Cesare, was there despite her death several years before. Chase is clear about how his mother influenced him, "My mother was full of fears ... the center of her life is her fears and preoccupations and everything else is on the periphery. The real world is on the periphery. And that's the way she was. She was not manipulative like Livia. And she wasn't, certainly, lethal like Livia. And she wasn't conniving ... she was narcissistic, she really was; and thought the worst all the time. So I was always scared about everything."[13] Much like his fictional alter-ego, Chase is plagued with self-doubt, dark thoughts, and aberrant fears.

Eyes Wide Open

This show has been recognized for its writing, acting, and true-to-life characters and has captured the fifth spot on *TV Guide*'s list of the best shows of all time. But not everyone loves *The Sopranos*. The Italian-American One Voice Committee gave Chase the "Pasta-tute" award for selling out his Italian-American heritage by cashing in on the depiction of Italian mob stereotypes. Others protest the explicit nature of the show. A disturbed viewer wrote this letter to HBO in disgust after viewing a third season episode: "For as long as I live, I will never forget the rape scene in last night's episode of *The Sopranos*. It was the ugliest, most disgusting, graphic and unnecessary rape scene I have ever seen ... [My wife] gagged, got up from her chair and announced that she would never watch another *Sopranos* episode and asked if I would mind if she canceled our HBO subscription—which your records will show we have had since day one."[14]

This kind of anger might seem justified. Without a doubt, *The Sopranos* is known for being violent and sexually explicit, unlike other shows that top the *TV Guide* list (*I Love Lucy* and *The Honeymooners*). Does the nature of this television show mean that it promotes violence? Lorraine Bracco (Dr. Melfi) says no. In an HBO Internet discussion, Bracco explains the positives of the brutal treatment of women in this TV drama; "Well, violence towards women, period, is despicable. What I like is that we don't pussyfoot around, and when you see violence for what it is, it's a huge deterrent. When you don't see violence and the person is already dead with the blood and they go onto the whole murder mystery part, I think it looks easy. It looks like nothing, and it feels like nothing, which is even worse. If people see violence and are revolted by it, maybe they wouldn't be so willing to do it."

Bracco is right. *The Sopranos* is reality TV. Not reality as in voyeuristic game shows, but as an accurate portrayal of a society where rape and violence is an actuality. Seeing the real story should make us sick and birth a yearning for justice, not a desire to mask the brutal reality. It is true that millions of viewers were sickened by the random brutality committed against a character that is loved and respected. But honorable women everywhere experience brutality and we choose to ignore it. Chase simply opens our eyes, and most of us hate what we see.

Let there be no doubt about the spiritual reality of these characters. When questioned about the eternal destiny of the loving and spiritual matriarch of the Soprano clan, Carmela, Chase replied, "She's the first one going to hell." Though unsure about the reality and nature of hell, he continues, "I don't mean that there was a guy with smoking horns. I mean that everyone in the show, that she [Carmela] has made this compromise to go along with this for her own agenda."[15] And this unreasonable selfishness is evil personified. It only seems palatable at times because it so closely reflects our own lives, and our own unspoken deals with the devil.

TONY SOPRANO
A NEO-SOLOMON FROM NEW JERSEY

Taking center stage in this Shakespearean-like tragicomedy is Tony Soprano, HBO's Don of New Jersey. This sometimes heroic, sometimes horrific fictional mob boss personifies every man's inner struggle. He is a physical portrait of the war that wages in the deep parts of all mankind, the great battle of redemptive good and despairing evil. He is a paradox of greatness and wretchedness. Stephen Holden from *The New York Times* agrees, "There are essentially two Tonys. One is a mobster ... the other is a straight-laced family man. The criminal Tony and a righteous Tony."[1] As the two are held in tension, we are held in tension.

Tony wasn't always a gangster. He was a typical grade school kid, a popular high school athlete, and a college student. But the lure of the family business was greater than the possibilities offered from traditional education. Tony wanted something more.

He is no simpleton. Tony is thoughtful, reflective, and often compassionate. We get a glimpse of this in the waiting room of Dr. Melfi's office. He could be reading a magazine, making phone calls, or counting his money, but instead he gazes thoughtfully at each work of art, and thinks. On one occasion he is deeply troubled by a small painting of a rural landscape with a red barn and a large tree. It aggravates him. In his session he offers an unsolicited response to the piece. Tony thinks it is a trick painting, a tool used by psychiatrists to lead their patients and create a response. He sees despair in a dilapidated barn and hollowed-out tree. Melfi sees nothing of the sort, no evidence of this in the painting. Obviously, Tony views this piece through his reality. Later he is captured by a portrait of the ocean and a beach house above his Russian girlfriend's bed and asks what it means to her. She sees no meaning, just a picture. This so-called Italian thug finds truth where many would find nothing. Tony looks deeper and sees more.

It is only fitting that around Tony Soprano's thick Italian neck hangs a gold chain bearing a pendant of Saint Jerome. Jerome, an Italian, was born in Italy 342 years after the birth of Jesus of Nazareth. Despite a Christian education and upbringing, Jerome neglected his faith and studied under a pagan in Rome. While mastering Greek and Latin he sowed his wild oats, living a life consumed with aberrant pleasures much like Tony Soprano. In a life-changing dream, Jerome sat before the judgment seat of God. God asked him, "Who are you?" He replied, "A Christian." But God corrected him: "You are a liar. You are not a Christian but a Ciceronian." Jerome was more clearly a follower of the Roman leader

Cicero and his ways than a follower of Christ and His ways. This realization was painful, and it changed Jerome's life. He awoke with a commitment to read the books of God passionately and serve his Creator faithfully.[2] He became the great translator of the Bible and a leader of the church.

It is interesting that Saint Jerome—a relatively obscure saint—is the image that lies over Tony's heart. Jerome can serve as a role model—a guide—calling the ruthless mobster into a new existence. Perhaps if Tony encountered God and was forced to face the truth about himself, he too would change drastically.

But Jerome isn't the only saint embraced by Tony. The patron saint of the Soprano family is Saint Peter, the forgiven betrayer of Jesus Christ. It is ironic, for betrayal is the ultimate sin in the world of organized crime.

Peter is a prominent figure in the brotherly ritual that ushers men into this criminal fraternity. In a small room hidden away from the world, men like young Christopher are initiated into the family. The men prick their fingers like ten-year-old boys in a secret club, burn the card of their patron saint, and repeat the rules and regulations in unison. As blood brothers, they pledge fidelity and obedience to this evil organization while the prayer card of Peter is enshrined in flames. As the card burns, they repeat the rules and regulations of the family and another man is "made."

Like Tony, this Apostle lives in extremes. Peter steps out of a boat and walks on water by faith, and then impulsively cuts a man's ear off out of fear.[3] One minute Jesus tells Peter he's the rock upon which the church will be built, and the next minute Jesus rebukes him sternly and says, "Get behind me, Satan!"[4] No wonder Tony can identify. In one scene he's playing Nintendo 64 and eating ice cream with his son, and the next he's murdering his best friend in a boat a few miles off the New Jersey coast.

The New Testament tells this story:

> Jesus pulled Peter to the side and with a somber tone informed him, "This very night, before the rooster crows, you will disown me three times." This was only a few hours before Jesus' execution. Peter was furious that Jesus could even think such a thing. He replied boldly, "Even if I have to die with you, I will never disown you." Later that night, Jesus was crucified. The next morning found Peter sitting in a courtyard scared and confused, wondering how God's son could be dead and thinking that he'd wasted several years of his life to follow a man who must have lied about who he really was. Jesus couldn't have been the Son of God; God would never allow such a tragedy. A young girl saw Peter in the courtyard and recognized him as a follower of Jesus. She asked, "Are you the man who knew the Jesus from Galilee?" He denied it. Another girl saw him and said to the people, "This man was a disciple of Jesus of Nazareth!" Again Peter denied it. Those standing there went up to Peter and said, "Your accent gives you away; surely you are one of them who followed

Jesus." Peter began to yell and curse and swear to those around him, "I do not know the man!" Immediately a rooster crowed.[5]

When the rooster crowed, Peter remembered Jesus saying, "You will disown me three times," and he wept bitterly. Later Peter repented and affirmed his love for Jesus, and Christ embraced him. Soon after, the church was in fact built on Peter. Luke wrote in the book of Acts, "in those days Peter stood up among the believers (a group numbering about a hundred and twenty)."[6]

It was Peter who stood up among the other apostles and led the church in its fragile, infant-like beginnings. Peter is the man who led 3,000 to faith by preaching one sermon, and 5,000 during another.[7] The same man authored two beautiful epistles in the New Testament and eventually was crucified upside down because he did not feel worthy to be murdered in the same way his God was. He was a bold man, ready to live and die for the family of faith.

Tony has spent his days silently disowning his Creator by the criminal life he leads. He has turned his back to the Almighty and refused to acknowledge the God who made man. But Tony has heard the rooster crow. Thoughts of death and impending doom, God, eternity, hell, and redemption have tattooed themselves inside the mind of New Jersey's lead Mafioso. Peter was the curious disciple, always seeking answers and always asking Jesus. Now Tony wants answers. Will he recognize his betrayal, and repent as his patron saint did? Or will he continue to be constantly plagued by the rooster's crow, hiding behind material wealth and power?

Indeed, the family business is more lucrative than ever. Tony could fit his childhood home into the basement of his Soprano mansion. Tony and Carmela take pleasure in the riches. They throw lavish parties, drive $80,000 cars, enjoy films in a state-of-the-art home theater, and dine in the finest restaurants. They deny themselves and their children nothing they desire. But it is the best of times, and it is the worst of times.

Tony is a modern day reflection of an ancient king, Solomon.

King Solomon, ruler of Israel circa 900 B.C., is quite possibly the most shocking of God's chosen leaders in the Bible, a book that is filled with the kind of deviant people who make up the Soprano crew. He is the son of King David and the godfather of Judaism. The Hebrew Scriptures describe him as the richest and wisest man to ever live. He ruled all, demonstrated astounding wisdom, wrote beautiful songs, and was loved by God. However, in spite of this divine favor, Solomon spent his life in search for meaning apart from God. He lived life in full pursuit of money, fame, and pleasure. His journey led him to accumulate great knowledge, build magnificent houses and vineyards, pursue sexual pleasure with a thousand of his closest friends, and become rich and powerful beyond measure. Yet all attempts at gratification end in vain. They are empty and soon take more than they give. "It is meaningless," Solomon said. "A chasing after the wind."[8]

When asked to describe *The Sopranos*, Michael Imperioli (Christopher Moltisanti) replied, "It's about an American man in his middle years who has had a certain degree of success, and his unhappiness with it."[9] The same could be said of Ecclesiastes (Solomon's poetic autobiography) with the simple substitution of "Hebrew man" for "American man." Solomon experienced a large degree of success and chronicled his sad, empty journey to alert future pleasure-seekers and warn them of its vanity.

Tony, like his biblical counterpart, is overwhelmed with a sense of meaninglessness. He has accumulated great wealth and power, yet feels poor and weak. He oversees an army of men who are committed to him and his cause (some more than others), yet feels alone and abandoned. He denies himself nothing, yet continues to live in emptiness and despair. He has money. Power. Strength. Influence. Success. With these things, however, he still cannot escape a life of depression, medication, instability, and alienation.

Humanity is fallen, bent the wrong way, seeking to constantly please the self. It believes happiness can be found in the material world. This is not true. Many people describe feeling cold and unfulfilled when reaching the pinnacle of their career. Tony describes this predicament in different terms: "I got the world by the balls, and I can't stop feeling like a fucking loser."

But peace and contentment are found only in the spiritual realm. To find it, man must be willing to stare into the abyss, ask the hard questions, and seek something outside of himself. Instead, most people divert themselves with the pursuit of the pleasures of this temporal world. This pursuit distracts us, until the futility of our lives becomes too much to bear.

Tony asks, "What's the point? You go to Italy, lift weights, watch a movie; it's all a series of distractions until you die." Henry David Thoreau understood this natural progression of depravity without repentance and wrote, "The masses of men lead lives of quiet desperation. What is called resignation is confirmed desperation ... A stereotyped but unconscious despair is concealed even under what are called the games and amusements of mankind."[10]

Christ described the things that make up our lives in two categories: the eternal and the temporal. The possessions of this world will burn, but no one can destroy your eternal wealth. As long as man blindly pursues the temporal and disregards the eternal, he will remain drowning in a sea of unfulfillment and despair. Try as he might, he will never find complete satisfaction. We all hear the familiar refrain: "I'll be happy when I reach this level of wealth, hold this, see this, know this, etc. When this happens, I'll be whole. I'll be complete."

But Ecclesiastes says, "The eye never has enough seeing, nor the ear its fill of hearing."[11] It is never enough, and that dream of being completely fulfilled now seems pointless; it is fleeting. Tony senses this and agrees with Solomon, "I'm like King Midas in reverse. Everything I touch turns to shit."

The conclusion of Solomon's journey is that life would be better if man would honor God and obey His teaching. This is a conclusion Tony Soprano has not reached, but is unmistakably journeying toward.

CARMELA SOPRANO
THE QUEEN OF THE CASTLE

Carmela is the queen of the castle in the Soprano kingdom. She is more than a caretaker. She manages the finances, cooks the meals, plans the social events, and rears the children. This intelligent woman does more than run the house; she nurtures everyone in it. Carmela is a forgiving wife, loving mother, encouraging friend, and practicing Catholic. Her name is appropriately derived from the Hebrew root word meaning "golden." Indeed, she is the only treasure that makes Tony a truly rich man. She sees her husband for the man he really is and loves him anyway. She has given herself fully to this family and is deeply loved and respected by both husband and children. But underneath this matriarchal symbol of perseverance and faith there is a "volcano of passion always threatening to erupt."[1]

J. Madison Davis, former president of The International Association of Crime Writers, North America, says it best, "In some ways, [Carmela] is tougher than Tony!"[2] She knows what she wants, and she knows how to get it. When facing the possibility that Meadow might go to college on the other coast, Carmela takes things into her own hands. She bakes a pie, gathers Meadow's academic records, and visits Jean Cusamano's sister, respected Georgetown alumna, insisting (very aggressively) she write Meadow a letter of recommendation to Georgetown. Carmela Soprano doesn't take "no" for an answer. Although Meadow doesn't end up at Georgetown, she goes to school on the East Coast at Columbia University, and Carmela gets her way.

The same is true at home. Carmela is not a weak woman who passively accepts Tony's marital infidelity. She confronts it, and calls it by name. When she sees Tony stare at another woman, she threatens his manhood saying, "If I had an ounce of self respect I'd cut your dick off." To avoid the potential disgrace of Tony fathering an illegitimate child, she directs her husband with force, "Listen, Tony, if you're gonna keep doing what you do, at the very least I want you to get a vasectomy. Let's get real, Tony. Do you have any idea what a bastard child would do to this family? Think of the shame." Carmela already has to compete with another "family" for Tony's loyalty; the last thing she needs is one more. Regarding a vasectomy Tony asks, almost jokingly, "Isn't it a sin to undo the good work God's done?" Carmela responds quickly, "Well, you should know; you've made a living of it." Tony finally concedes and goes under the knife. Although Carmela doesn't make him go through with the procedure, it is clear that Tony loves this woman and will do what she asks.

Her beauty is stunning and her strength is entrancing.

Carmela could have married another man and avoided the complications that come with being Mrs. Soprano. Tony could suddenly disappear to avoid prosecution, or could be incarcerated and lose any ability to father his children. Carmela knows the risks. But it is clear she loves Tony and will give everything she has to be with him.

Carmela does take pleasure in the luxuries Tony's profession provides. Torn between her desire for spiritual wellness, her love for her husband, and the means by which he provides for their family, Carmela is stuck in the middle of a difficult dilemma—an inner struggle between her desire for comfort and security, and a living conscience that knows real people die to make her luxurious lifestyle possible. One day she basks in the glow of a $20,000 fur coat, and the next it seems she finally resolves to leave Tony. She has good reason to leave. Tony is unfaithful, and his lifestyle places both him and their family in constant jeopardy of prosecution or mortal harm. But the reason she stays is clear: She loves him. It is not for the money, the house, or the cars. It is the depressed, nocturnal mob boss she vowed to love, honor, and cherish. One thing is certain: Carmela is committed to the family.

The Faith of Carmela Soprano

"God delights in concealing things."—Proverbs 25:23

Tony's wife of twenty years manages to balance her firm religious beliefs and her taxing role as a mob wife. She wants to mature spiritually and be a better Catholic, but only gets marginal help on her spiritual journey from the church. She raises her deep questions about Christ and the Bible to her priest, "I understand what Jesus did, but a lot of what He said I don't get. Like, the sun rises on the just and the unjust alike. Why?"

A great mystery surrounds the word of God, a very magical unknown that entrances those who listen and provokes a response from all who hear. Jesus spoke to His disciples saying, "[God] causes his sun to rise on the evil and the good, and sends rain on the righteous and the unrighteous."4 Carmela is confounded by this passage, "Does that mean whores get into heaven before the righteous?" The disciples were puzzled too and wondered how God, who delights in good and shuns evil, could offer the same grace of sunlight and raindrops to all men, the righteous and the unrighteous alike. Carmela and the disciples ponder the enigma of a God who blesses all and offers grace to the multitudes. Many can identify.

When Scripture speaks, it awakens more questions than it answers. At once it offers a key and you are enlightened by its wisdom; you are given access through a locked door. Then, in an instant, that door reveals other doors and other mysteries to be explored, too many to count.

Annie Dillard says of nature, "[It] is very much a now-you-see-it, now-you-don't affair. A fish flashes, then dissolves in the water before my eyes like so much salt. Deer apparently ascend bodily into heaven; the brightest oriole fades into leaves. These disappearances stun me into stillness and concentration; they say of nature that it conceals with a grand nonchalance, and they say of vision that it is a deliberate gift, the revelation of a dancer who for my eyes only flings away her seven veils. For nature does reveal as well as conceal: now-you-see-it, now-you-don't."[5]

The same is true with the word of God. It stuns people into stillness and concentration. It conceals with a grand nonchalance. It offers vision as a deliberate gift. For Scripture does reveal as well as conceal. "Now-you-see-it, now-you-don't." Christ was a brilliant storyteller who spoke in riddles and parables, frequently capturing His audience in paradox. He confounded people with statements like, "The last will be first, and the first will be last."[6] And, "Whoever finds his life will lose it, and whoever loses his life for my sake will find it."[7]

In these riddles, the answers Carmela seeks are not easily found. So when things get tough, Carmela goes shopping. Tony may divert himself with Prozac and women, but his wife buys clothes and furniture. The counsel of Christ goes against natural fallen instincts. He said, "A man's life does not consist in the abundance of his possessions."[8] In fact, Christ said, "Do not worry about your life, what you will eat, or about your body, what you will wear. Life is more than food, and the body more than clothes."[9] Spiritual matters must become more important than the physical. The things of the spirit give life; possessions ignite only a fleeting pleasure.

Consider these scandalous words spoken by Christ that Carmela addresses to her priest, "When you give a luncheon or dinner, do not invite your friends, your brothers or relatives, or your rich neighbors; if you do, they may invite you back and so you will be repaid. But when you give a banquet, invite the poor, the crippled, the lame, the blind, and you will be blessed. Although they cannot repay you, you will be repaid at the resurrection of the righteous."[10] This doesn't sit well with a wealthy woman who displays her home like a trophy to the upper crust of New Jersey. The words of Christ make it difficult for people to call themselves Christians.

This tension between biblical truth and the reality of Carmela's life has invoked some strange behavior. The seduction of her priest. A near affair with a home repairman. And the escape of her outlandish spending. Most of us live like this sometimes-devout wife of a mob boss, longing to live out the spiritual truth we have been taught and remaining confused about the rest. Carmela is not alone on her journey.

"You know the value of prayer: it is precious beyond all price. Never, never neglect it."—Sir Thomas Buxton[11]

THE PRAYER OF CARMELA

While young Christopher lies motionless in the ICU, the gangsters surrounding him turn to faith. The young Mafioso, shot through the chest by ambitious underlings, is helpless and left in the hands not of his doctors, but his Creator. The hospital gown, brandished with the image of Pope John Paul II, himself the survivor of near fatal wounds from an assassin's firearm, replaces the suit and tie of New Jersey's rising criminal star. As the outlandish family hovers in the waiting room, they remind one another to do one thing: pray. No doubt each one is reaching out to the divine. Even A.J. claims to be praying while simultaneously playing video games. But it is the maternal prayer of Carmela Soprano that captures the moment with devotion and utter sincerity. Crisis has broken the façade of her convenient faith, and in desperation she turns to God, prays a beautiful prayer of confession, and begs for God's intervention in the life of her families.

Gentle and Merciful Lord Jesus

The Father grants grace through his son. Therefore, effective prayer centers on Christ and is integrated into a life of faith and love for God. Carmela knows this and prays to Christ on Christopher's behalf. She pleads to the divine, begging for a miracle. She wants Christopher to live and knows the only way for him to be restored is by the power of Christ. She prays honestly and openly for his survival.

An Open Heart ... An Honest Heart

Carmela speaks truth to her all-knowing Creator. There is no pretense or illusion given in this prayer. She opens her heart, confessing her need for intervention. If Christopher is to be spared, Carmela knows she must "approach the throne of grace with confidence" and sincerity.[12] Many turn communication with the divine into a forced exercise of language instead of an honest conversation with the one who created man's very soul. C.S. Lewis said, "We must lay before Him what is in us, not what ought to be in us."[13]

Take My Sins and the Sins of my Family

Her prayer is not far from the Psalmist's who cried, "O Lord, have mercy on me; heal me, for I have sinned against you."[14] It is merely directed outward, for Christopher and for her family. She acknowledges God's mercy and forgiveness and confesses her sins, trusting in the hands of the Lord. When faced with choosing three years of famine, three months of being swept away by his enemies, or three days of plague in the land, King David pleaded, "I am in deep distress. Let me fall into the hands of the Lord, for his mercy is very great."[15] In deep distress, Carmela opens her heart to Christ, confessing her sin, and begging for forgiveness. She is well aware of her sin.

In Full Awareness of the Consequences

Carmela accepts her own responsibility in this matter before God, and requests the forgiveness Christ came to give. She received Tony's hand in marriage knowing full well the life she was committing to. And Christopher knows the stakes as well. They have chosen a life contrary to the Christian life, a life supported by sin and criminal activities. But she confesses. Carmela longs for the gap between her and her Creator to be bridged, a gap that was made by her sinful choices.

If it is Your Will

She knows God's plan will be accomplished on earth as it is in heaven.[16] But she also believes Scripture when it says, "You do not have, because you do not ask."[17] So she asks in faith for God to act and save this young man whom she and Tony love like a son. She prays in confidence for the Maker of heaven and earth to heal and restore. And she prays not only for this, but for vision and insight as well.

May He See Your Love

This is a wonderful prayer. What could be better for anyone than to clearly see who God is, and to sense the love of the great Storyteller of redemption? Carmela desires Christopher to see his sin and repent. David prayed, "My sins have overtaken me, and I cannot see."[18] Our sin blinds us and prevents us from seeing the truth. It weakens our vision and prevents us from gaining insight into our lives, which desperately need direction. This type of prayer is crucial to our journey. Hank Hanegraaff affirms, "Prayer is the Christian life, reduced to its essence."[19]

Like Carmela, most people resort to prayer merely in times of crisis. Yet, the peace and power she found kneeling beside a hospital bed is constantly accessible to all of God's creation. When prayer and meditation become an integrated part of a diverse life, the cares of this world fade and joy is renewed. A monastic follower of Christ devoted to prayer and contemplation, Brother Lawrence taught, "In order to form a habit of conversing with God continually, and referring all we do to Him, we must at first apply to Him with some diligence: but that after a little care we should find His love inwardly excite us to it without any difficulty."[20] In other words, the discipline of prayer and meditation will become such a delight that this life of devotion becomes natural and easy.

Oswald Chambers said, "Prayer does not fit us for the greater work; prayer is the greater work."[21] Many long to become more spiritual so they might become more skilled and devoted to prayer. But it is prayer, a space devoted to being in the presence of the Almighty, which makes us more spiritual. There is no substitute. Knowledge will not lead to the heart of God; it only "puffs up."[22] The only authentic path to peace is to travel the road of contemplative prayer.

True and honest prayer is a starting place in genuine faith for Carmela Soprano. The words she prays for young Christopher are truthful and beautiful, but she should also pray them for herself, that she would have vision to see her own spiritual reality, and break free from the sin that plagues her. Blaming Tony has grown old; she has chosen this life and all that goes with it, and it has been destroying her. Her children see her hypocrisy and a day is coming when she will have to choose a path that follows the God whom she speaks of so often. Jesus described this path as narrow and difficult; many will be unwilling to travel this long hard road. Like the rich young ruler who Christ asked to sell all that he had to follow Him, Mrs. Soprano will have to either abandon her luxurious lifestyle and follow God or abandon her faith. A stern and wise therapist contextualized this challenge, advising Carmela to live only on Tony's honest earnings and not on the rewards of his lies and deceit. She is seeking truth, and her choice may shake the foundations of this criminal underworld.

MEADOW AND A.J. SOPRANO
THE CHILDREN

The children of the most powerful criminal in New Jersey live an almost normal suburban life. Except for the hidden guns and wads of cash concealed inside fake soup cans, their home life seems quite ordinary. Meadow and A.J. love one another and get along very well. They have formed an alliance that protects them from their father's unfaithfulness. After all, Tony has pledged that his criminal family will always come first, before his own wife and children. This seems scandalous, but the honesty is almost refreshing. Many men put their vocation before all else, but will never admit it. Vacation days spent for children's births, recitals, ball games, and birthdays are seen as an inconvenience, a distraction from the ascent up the professional ladder. Tony and his cohorts only state the obvious: Greed and power are even more paramount than family.

Meadow

In many ways Meadow is just like any other teenage daughter. She romanticizes about boys and relationships. She worries about school and her future. She questions her parents' methods of discipline and correction and is bothered by her brother's invasions of her privacy. Meadow does, however, have unique issues of her own. Only a Soprano kid would find $50,000 in Krugerrands and a .45 automatic while hunting for Easter eggs. She bears the burden of two families, but Meadow proves herself to be strong when dealing with the pressures of both.

After facing the embarrassment of walking through the door with her friends while the FBI is searching their home and leading her father out handcuffed, Meadow says to Carmela, "That's who Dad is. My friends don't judge me. And fuck them if they do. I'll cut them off." This smart, beautiful, and forthright young lady knows just how to do that. If a friend or parent crosses her, she withdraws completely from the relationship and takes control. Meadow knows the reason people are drawn to her: She is much more than a pretty face. She is a scholar, an athlete, and a gifted singer.

Throughout the series, Meadow confronts hard issues and presses ahead for answers. Racism, the existence of God, sex and sexuality, right and wrong: these things and others are engaged and explored. She appears to be disinterested in spiritual matters, but is reaching a crisis point after the death of her former boyfriend and criminal cousin, Jackie Junior. She masks the pain of his loss with vodka and tries to laugh through the pain. But this Columbia University freshman is drowning in despair. The reality of her father's business and the violence that surrounds it is telling a story she does not want to hear. Can she hide from this grim reality and enjoy the lavish life she has grown accustomed to like her mother? Or will she leave the material trappings of her mob family for safety and integrity?

Meadow is not clueless about the family business. She plainly questions her dad about his involvement in the mafia. Meadow longs for the curtain to be lifted on the mystery of her family and will not stop until the answers are found. Tony tells her the truth, and later rubs the truth in her face by offering her an SUV that belonged to a high school classmate. Tony took the car in lieu of payment for her classmate's father's gambling debts. Meadow is not amused, and Tony makes his point. Everything they have comes from his criminal profession: the cars, house, food, computers, and clothes. If she doesn't like it, she can turn in her Discover card.

Like her parents, she has learned to be a survivor. When considering where to direct his parenting efforts Tony admits, "I'm not worried about Meadow. She can take care of herself." And she does. There is no doubt Meadow is a Soprano.

A.J.

The heir to the Mafioso throne is an overweight, problematic student who spends his time playing video games and downloading porn from the Internet. He has an explosive temper and a foul mouth and is prized by his peers. Sound familiar? He is a chip off the old block. In fact, you can almost rest assured that after thirty years of syndication, The Sopranos will return to HBO in 2030 with Anthony Junior as the new boss of New Jersey.

The similarities are not lost on Tony. He often lashes out against his son in moments of disgust. Tony articulates to Dr. Melfi the tension of being a mobster and father to A.J., "I want him to be proud of me. I just don't want him to be like me." Whether A.J. can handle his father's verbal attacks and step into manhood has yet to be seen. The cute irresponsibility of adolescence is overworn. Boys will be boys, but getting drunk on sacramental wine, defecating in the school pool, and smoking marijuana at your own confirmation are deplorable acts. His behavior is not even acceptable in a mob family.

His personality is so naïve that the rebellion does not seem purposeful, but his actions are speaking louder than words. The chaos of his two families has called everything into question. He is unsure about faith, family, who he is, and quite certainly who he will become. He is no longer a boy and is not yet a man. His father has said he could never make it in the business but he shows little promise as a scholar. So A.J. makes friends and pursues anything that seems fun, but never prepares for or speaks of his future. Many young men dream of becoming firemen, MTV veejays, or baseball players, but A.J. lacks any sign of true aspiration.

There are numerous answers when it comes to potential solutions for A.J. His father believes military school would toughen him up and teach him discipline. His school counselors recommend specialized teaching and therapy for a borderline case of Attention Deficit Disorder. The school psychologist diagnoses this based upon four random behaviors: "He often has difficulty awaiting his turn, is often 'on the go' or acts as if driven by a motor; often interrupts or intrudes on others, and often fidgets with hands or feet." If there were a prepubescent schoolboy in existence who did not exhibit these behaviors, it would be a surprise.

Tony and Carmela cannot agree on how to handle their son. Neither is impressed with A.J.'s efforts socially or academically. Fearful of the kind of man he will become, they search for answers, but they do not come easily. Tony's solution is simple, "He just needs a slap upside the head." And so does Tony. Instead, he soothes himself with Lithium, Prozac, and a therapist who will not call a spade a spade. Interestingly, Tony knows what kind of discipline his son needs, because his son is a clear reflection of his own faults. What neither needs is a psychological diagnosis that only masks the problem.

RAISING KIDS IN AN INFORMATION AGE

The perfect family is the chimera of American life, existing only as a pretense, a false reality many hope for and project outwardly, though most inwardly realize it is one they will never achieve. I speak of children and parenting with great humility, knowing that as a father of two young girls, many mistakes will mark my path. Because young souls are so fragile, they can be crushed by the abrupt force of a father or flourish under the loving provision of a mindful parent. It is awe-inspiring that a human life is entrusted to two people, for rearing a child is the most daunting task undertaken by a man or woman. Yet this is the nature of being a parent. It means accepting a beautiful gift from God, without any impression of actual preparedness, and choosing to give one's self wholly to the task.

Family therapist Augustus Y. Napier writes, "Parenting is a profoundly reciprocal process: we, the shapers of our children's lives, are also being shaped. As we struggle to be parents, we are forced to encounter ourselves, and if we are willing to look at what is happening between us and our children, we may learn how we came to be who we are."[1] In the same way, Tony and Carmela are growing as their children grow. Their offspring are the tools God is using to refine them and to teach them about selfless love.

In many ways Tony relates to his kids because he's just an overgrown child himself. His wife asks him and demands to know, "Why don't you grow the fuck up?" Good question. This man sleeps during the day and gets in trouble with his friends and girlfriend at night. (Sounds like the college experience he never had.) Yet this overrun mobster and his wife are given the remarkable opportunity to guide their children, while continually being shaped and molded into better people. They are given a glimpse into their heritage and into their future while their home is graced with youthfulness. They are parenting and learning who they really are.

Children mimic what they see; they observe behavior and follow by example. This is how they learn. The challenge then of being a parent is offering our children a life worthy of imitation. For example, A.J. offers the same respect to Carmela as Tony offers to Livia, and Meadow imitates the way her parents deal with conflict. She explodes in anger, buries her frustration, or runs.

However, don't believe Tony and Carmela are all bad. The most important foundation for children to possess is the unconditional love of a parent. And this is Tony Soprano's greatest accomplishment. He has broken a generational cycle of neglect and emotional detachment in his family and has offered unwavering affection to his children. His family is dysfunctional, of course. He brings cold-blooded killers into his home and his children refer to them as uncles. This is not an ideal environment for young children. But as Scripture says, "Love covers over a multitude of sins."[2] Tony deeply loves his children, and they know it. It shows.

Scripture says, "He who loves [his son] is careful to discipline him."[3] The Bible is clear on how parental love and care manifest themselves in the family. Tony and Carmela know that discipline is important in rearing a child, but like most parents they feel weak and helpless. Their parents did not model the skills they need to raise children, and it is clear they are making their own path, searching for something that will work. Tony articulates this despair to Carmela while trying to figure out how to punish Meadow for hosting a party with drugs and alcohol at her grandmother's empty house, "If she finds out we're powerless, we are fucked." He also enforces A.J.'s punishment after A.J. gets drunk on sacramental wine at school, but offers encouragement and good advice to his moping son, telling him, "You're not depressed. You're sad and you're angry 'cause you did something stupid and you got grounded." As Tony sees his son hit bottom he affirms him by making them both sundaes and starting a playful food fight with whipped cream and nuts. The smoke and mirrors of mob life are gone, and all you see is a beautiful picture of a father and his son.

•

Meadow disparages the lack of parental responsibility all too common today, as seen in the Aprile family. Jackie Junior is dead, shot through the head by a mobster that took orders from Jackie Junior's father several years before. Not even the loyalty to his father's memory can pay the price to save the life of this college-flunkey-turned-drug-frenzied gunman. Meadow not only blames her criminal family, but more specifically Jackie's parents who gave their son no direction. Their parenting philosophy was "laissez faire," complete freedom with no discipline, reproof, or correction. The proverbs of the Old Testament speak to this parenting philosophy, saying, "He who spares the rod hates his son, but he who loves him is careful to discipline him."[4] Meadow recalls the sorrow Jackie possessed because he was totally free. His parents did not question, restrict, or train him. They didn't care. This child left to raise himself is now dead before his twentieth birthday. Jackie Junior grew up in the command center of mob activity, and his father was the boss until his early death due to cancer. Tony promised Jackie Senior he would see that his son would steer clear of mob life. But Tony's attempts were too little, too late for a young man wandering through life without the guidance of his elders. From childhood on through adolescence Jackie Junior grew up like many American youth, rich in material possessions and poor in regards to love, direction, and encouragement. Parents who ignore the need for children to have boundaries that distinguish right from wrong will reap a lifetime of sorrow.

It should be noted that discipline is often mislabeled abuse, and vice versa. Tony's parents didn't train him; they abused him with words and fists. Tony confesses to Dr. Melfi, "Dad would smack us kids around." It seems Tony has moved beyond his upbringing and is giving his children a life better than his own, until A.J. is expelled from school and Tony slaps his son in rage. This is not how to "train a child in the way he should go."[5] It is venting one's own anger and frustration on a young person who does not know how to take it.

Tony generally knows when he has sinned against his son. After a vulgar tirade where he humiliates his own son, mocking him as his only male heir, Tony returns humbly to his son and apologizes, "I'm sorry for talking to you the way I did. I was wrong and I hope you know I didn't mean it." A.J. perks out of a slump as his father's kind words heal the pain of his accusations. Then Tony says to his son what every son longs to hear, "I couldn't ask for a better son, A.J., and I mean that." The one man that makes all the difference, his dad, loves him. This is how it is with Tony Soprano, a deeply flawed man with a great love for his children.

THE SINS OF THE FATHER
ARE PASSED TO THE SON

In contrast to what Dr. Melfi says about "genetic predispositions" (they are only predispositions and not determining factors), the Old Testament speaks severely of the generational consequences of sin. Sons are punished for their father's deeds, or to say it another way, the sins of the father are passed to the son. This scriptural counsel is visibly played out in the Soprano family. The actions of a father have powerful consequences on following generations, from Tony's father, Johnny Boy, to Tony, and from Tony to Anthony Junior.

Anthony Junior is more than a class clown at his private Catholic school. His junior high rap sheet is beyond belief. Along with the usual teenage rebellion, it includes vandalism, theft, and drunkenness, all in grand fashion. He doesn't just get drunk at school; A.J. steals the sacramental wine that symbolizes Jesus' atonement of sins. Stealing from the church, as Carmela says, is as low as it gets. The principal and school psychologist believes they have identified A.J.'s problems. They say he has trouble following the rules, weighing consequences, and thinking before he acts. These, they assert, are possible symptoms of a disease, not just youthful indiscretion. To Tony, whose face turned pale after hearing the list of symptoms, all of which he himself possesses, it sounds like a natural result of the Soprano gene pool. A.J. is simply carrying on the family name.

The reality that A.J. will follow in his father's footsteps could not be clearer. The similarities are astounding. Dr. Melfi asks Tony concerning his son, "Do you see his behavior as a reflection of your own?" There is no response. The words just hang in the air, unanswered. Tony wants to believe there's a way out for his son, but how can he? He doesn't even believe there was a way out for himself. In one session Tony admits, "You're born to this shit. You are what you are."

As Tony becomes aware of the traits he will inevitably bequeath to Anthony Junior, memories of his own father's sin begin to fill his mind. Tony's father was not the saint his mother laments. Tony remembers watching his father attack a man, throwing him to the ground, kicking him in the ribs, and smashing a flowerpot over his head. Later Tony saw his father being handcuffed and dragged away by the police right before his eyes.

Mr. Satriale may have been a poor gambler who couldn't pay his debts, but did Tony's father really have to go to such extreme measures? Tony walked in just in time to see his dad cut off this feeble butcher's pinkie; this was Johnny Boy's attempt to collect on money owed. As a result, a nine-year-old boy sees the world and the free meat on his table in a new light. Every slice of cheese and cappicola is taken from a butcher with only nine fingers. And Tony knows why. His subconscious will not let him forget the terror of his childhood, the sin of his father, the price paid for the food he puts in his mouth. Even as a grown man, the sight of sausage on the grill or sandwich meat in the refrigerator can send this 300-pound gangster to the floor in an unconscious slumber.

Tony regularly inflicts more tragedy than merely removing a small digit; he takes bolt cutters to the groin of a Hasidic tough guy, threatening to squeeze tight and cut if he doesn't comply. This makes a pinkie seem expendable. Tony chooses to embrace his father and the gangster lifestyle and now may be reaping what he sowed. He does not love the violence he feared as a child, he is tortured with dreams of the night he killed Matthew Bevalaqua, but this is the life he knew, the life of his father. Dr. Melfi's question pierces Tony to the core: "Do you hold your father responsible for what you've become?"

Tony was confronted with a dilemma: reject your own father and his criminal behavior, push aside the man that provides for you and whom you've elevated as a hero, or embrace him and inevitably become like him. Incapable of weighing the consequences of this greed gone mad, he must make a choice that shapes who he is and who he will become. Tony is forced to choose: reject, push aside, or embrace. Likewise, A.J. does not understand the full implications of what his father does for a living. He is oblivious to the fact that his father murdered Pussy, A.J.'s godfather, to protect and maintain a life of crime.

Tony feels the full weight of Anthony Junior's past, present, and future mistakes. He hopes A.J. can be something better, but he must be realistic. As he retraces the steps of his father, Dr. Melfi reminds him, "You say you like The History Channel. He who doesn't understand history is doomed to repeat it." Tony could leave the life, atone for his father's mistakes, and offer Anthony Junior something better. But he will not, and so he asks his psychiatrist in despair, "My son is doomed, right?"

Is there any reason to belabor the indiscretions of an adolescent youth? Whatever happened to "boys will be boys"? It is assumed this is accepted behavior. While engaging in conversation around the dinner table about A.J.'s suspension, Livia spills the beans on Tony: He was the same way. Junior quickly adds that Tony was a hellion who used to steal cars and fence goods at the age of ten.

Obviously, Tony was no angel. The truth of his rebellion and sin is evident; it is all over the house. The expensive paintings on the walls, the home theater system with surround sound, and the free meat that sits before them speak of Tony's life choice. That is the point. Tony gave away his dreams of college and legitimate business before he even began his teenage years. He is a Soprano, after all. And despite efforts to leave a life of crime and greed, in the Soprano house the family name means something. And in this family, values are passed down from generation to generation.

FAMILY VALUES: GREED, CONSUMERISM, AND RACISM

Greed

Money makes this world go around.

Cold hard cash appears everywhere on *The Sopranos*: hidden in imitation soup cans in the pantry; buried in the basement; hidden in the walls; and in a huge wad in Tony's front pocket. It buys inside information from the police, keeps Carmela happy, endows Columbia University, and keeps the gangsters on the street earning. No one even stops long enough to question the deep love of money that drives the despicable behavior on this show. What do material possessions offer that make it worth the torment of continual participation in this criminal lifestyle? What do riches bring that drown out morality's cry? St. Paul writes, "The love of money is a root of all kinds of evil."[1] However, it seems in *The Sopranos* the love of money is the root of all kinds of pleasure; it covers over a multitude of sins. For example, if you kill a man, and nothing is gained, it was a bad business move. But if you kill a man, and you pocket four grand, the murder is justified. The love of money covers over a multitude of sins. Tony is caught in the tension. He sees the evil that greed brings with it, yet continues to feast on its spoils.

Dante lamented the sin of his fair Italian city, Florence, asserting in *De Monarchia*, "Greed is the extreme opposite of justice."[2] Aristotle said, "Take away greed completely and nothing opposed to justice remains in the will."[3] The prophetic rebuke of Dante is still needed today. He spoke with truth and sorrow over the state of his country, "A glut of self-made men and quick-got gain. Have bred excess in thee and pride, forsooth, O Florence! Till e'en now thou criest for pain."[4] Greed leads a people to the brink of destruction and far away from God.

When an old high school friend wants to gamble at Tony's illegal high stakes card game, Tony discourages it at first, but eventually gives in knowing the credit he extended his friend could be multiplied by bankrupting his sporting goods business. He tries to do the right thing, but remains the chief of sinners. Like the Apostle Paul, the things he does not want to do, he does.[5] His conscience is overtaken by his greed. Although Tony lives the high life in upper-middle class New Jersey, he would ruin a man's life to earn a little extra cash. Jesus warned the crowd, "Watch out! Be on your guard against all kinds of greed. A man's life does not consist in the abundance of his possessions."[6]

Yet, in this show, everyone's being paid off: the police, the FBI, the informants, and not least of all, Carmela. Like her therapist advised, her priest counsels her to stay with her husband but to make major changes, "You say your husband has good in him. What you have to do is learn to live on what the good part earns." She then prepares herself to live a frugal life with Tony. Later Tony notices Carmela is not wearing her new $10,000 ring. She lies and says the ring is getting sized. She wants to be a good person, do what's right, but the change is difficult. If she revolts and chooses to live a simple life she will be stripped of her diversions and be forced to face her own reality, not liking what she sees. And greed is a powerful motivator, leading one on a path of material wealth but further away from spiritual fulfillment.

Consumerism

Everyone must eat and find shelter, so we consume. It is one thing to consume in order to live, and something altogether different to live to consume. Consumerism has become the ethos of the American life. This lifestyle runs completely contrary to the Judeo-Christian ethic. Rabbi and social justice advocate Tsvi Blanchard speaks about Jewish tradition of "consecrated consumption," the spiritual discipline of living life unto God and not our possessions.[7]

Western Christians assume that capitalism is right, even biblical. The early church fathers could not disagree more vehemently. "Business is in itself an evil," Augustine charged.[8] And Jerome (the saint worn around Tony's neck) suspected, "A man who is a merchant can seldom if ever please God."[9] The accumulation of wealth by people of faith would be considered scandalous when widows and orphans suffered. Interestingly, today families led by women make up the majority of people in poverty. While 65 percent of the world's production comes from women, they earn 20 percent of the world's income and yet possess only 2 percent of the means of production.[10] Early church leaders would never sanction this kind of economy.

We live in a society in which profit supercedes people. If I make money, who cares if other people are hurt? It happened with Enron. It happens when billion dollar companies go to under-developed countries and hire child laborers to work for twelve cents an hour. It's greed pure and simple that compels us to chase after wealth no matter what the cost to others. And our sinful desire to satisfy our selfish wants is never satisfied. Solomon's wisdom is truer now than ever: "Whoever loves money never has money enough; whoever loves wealth is never satisfied with his income."[11] We consume and consume, never having our fill, but always wanting more. Psychologist Enrich Fromm writes, "Greed is a bottomless pit which exhausts the person in an endless effort to satisfy the need without ever reaching satisfaction."[12] Consumers are taught foremost that appetite is insatiable and freedom of choice is invaluable. Tony Soprano personifies Fromm's statement. He exhausts himself in his search for temporal treasures, to the point of anxiety, or even to the point of passing out, "without ever reaching satisfaction." He has reached a peak in accumulating wealth, yet remains unsatisfied and continues to pillage New Jersey because he can never get enough.

Jesus said, "Do not store up for yourselves treasures on earth, where moth and rust consume and where thieves break in and steal, but store up for yourselves treasures in heaven."[13]

Men work and work and work to buy all sorts of trendy appliances and clever tools and designer furniture and the finest foods and fastest cars to fill their homes, their garages, their offices, their bellies. This is the American dream. Work. Buy. Display. Repeat. We consume and waste resources while the rest of the world struggles for air under an ocean of poverty. Years ago consumption was known as a disease of the lungs that forced you to fight for oxygen. Now it is considered an accolade given to those who drive the economy of American wealth.

Racism

It should be noted that Tony Soprano does not consider himself white; he is Italian. He won't let you forget it. He mocks the Anglo population who eat Sunday gravy out of a jar (Italians call it gravy, not sauce). Celebrating the beauty of Italian culture, *The Sopranos* pontificate about the gifts shared by "al paesans": pasta, pizza, espresso, and the telephone (invented by Antonio Meucci, not Alexander Graham Bell).

Every ethnic group should love the things that make them unique, but a line is crossed when one goes beyond loving his own culture and begins disparaging people of other ethnicities. You can't watch fifteen minutes of *The Sopranos* without catching a racial slur or derogatory comment about Jews, African-Americans, Hispanics, and other minorities. The words "Mulignan," "Smoke," and "Ditzoon" are used frequently to describe African Americans. Sometimes the slurs are meant to be comical, like when Tony tells the Jamaican woman caring for his mom, "No ganja while you're here." But when he is pulled over by a black cop Tony lets his anger loose, calling the officer an "affirmative action cock sucker." Tony's philosophy is made clear when he catches Meadow on the couch snuggling with her African American/Jewish boyfriend, Noah. "You stick with your own kind," Tony tells this boy in a very rough and vulgar fatherly tone. That is what Tony believes. You don't mix with other races.

Greed, consumerism, and racism: I wouldn't call them family values. But this is the state of the Soprano household, a family that reflects values all too familiar in suburban America.

CONFIRMED IN THE FAITH

At some point in life a choice is made and fate is established. People arrive at a crossroads, and the path they choose determines the rest of their journey. Some call it destiny or providence. Others call it chance.

When Christopher comes to his crossroads, he finds himself torn by competing desires. He dreams of being a "made" man, yet longs to be a Hollywood player. At A.J.'s confirmation party, Tony confronts Christopher and offers him the choice to stay with the family and be completely loyal or walk away and never return. Those are his options: to be a West Coast player or an East Coast gangster. The two cannot coexist. A choice must be made; he must follow one path and abandon another.

Earlier, just before his confirmation in faith, the youngest Soprano exclaims, "God is dead." Anthony Junior has sipped from the well of postmodern philosophy and neither his mother nor his priest can bring him back to a childlike faith.

Given the chaos of his own life, the ideas of Nietzsche seem to ring true. God must be dead or life would not feel so meaningless or difficult or painful. The pagan postmodern rhetoric of Anthony Junior alarms Tony and Carmela. The fact A.J. wrecked his mother's $80,000 Mercedes pales in comparison to this "no God shit" (as Tony put it).

Tony holds on here to the vestiges of religion, but only to what suits him: his Catholic heritage and enough religious upbringing for his children to keep Carmela happy. Clearly, the way A.J. is deconstructing the western modern world seems suspect and overtly radical because it threatens to change the way Tony sees everything. Tony himself wades through the malaise of postmodernity every day. The terms of French philosophers are unfamiliar, but the worldview fits perfectly, like a snug winter coat. He rejects moral absolutes. Murder, for instance, is acceptable during war, and in this criminal life they are like soldiers. Therefore, even homicide is not a sin. The moral relativism offered by postmodernity is a mantra in this criminal underworld. In their unique context they have allowed right and wrong to be vanquished by metaphors of war and duty.

Dr. Melfi explains the origin of postmodern thought exemplified by Nietzsche, Derrida, Foucault, and others as a European philosophy. After World War II people were cynical and became overwhelmed by the atrocities, sparking the philosophy that there are no absolute truths. The modern belief was that progress and technology were making us better, but the Holocaust proved nothing could be further from the truth. Mankind chose to use the advancement of science to bring evil to new heights, and the basic tenets of civilization were now in question. The Soprano household knows this same tension. Things that should be true in every culture (i.e. motherly instincts to love and nurture) are absent here; Livia Soprano is more likely to wound and kill. When motherly love is not true, everything else is up for grabs.

Anthony Junior is not trying to torment his mother with difficult questions about faith and existence; he is hoping someone can offer truth and explain the futility of life. Dr. Melfi defines this as a difficult dilemma for A.J., "When some people first realize that they are solely responsible for their own decisions, actions, and beliefs, and that death lies at the end of every road, they can be overcome by intense dread, a dull, aching anger that leads them to conclude that the only absolute truth is death."

A.J. ponders his own purpose in life, saying, "Do you ever think, 'Why were we born?'" He is searching for anything on this earth that has meaning. Life is absurd and death only proves the point. Meadow quotes French novelist and essayist Madame De Stael, "In life one must choose between boredom and suffering." Life is painful, and we either face the pain and suffering or divert ourselves from the turmoil and detach through one medium or another. This is the apex of truth apart from God. If there is no Creator of heaven and earth seeking out mankind in order to know and love them, then this is the best-case scenario. But just as King Solomon found, there is meaning. It is found in the spiritual realm, not the material. Anthony Junior passes through the rite of full acceptance into the church, God's community, yet finds no spiritual meaning. In fact, he is quick to divert himself from the pain with drugs. He is looking for spiritual truth, participates in the church initiation, and finds a complete void where he hopes to find answers. He is not seeking religion; this is a young boy who longs to know truth and to experience peace.

Strangely enough, A.J. may be the most spiritually mature individual on this show. His mother knows he is not a good Catholic and questions him about the kind of animal that smokes marijuana at his confirmation. This is not the response of a young man who has entered the church of St. Peter, it is the cry of a young man who longs to forget the emptiness of the religious ritual he experienced. He is mature because he is seeking answers to the mysteries of life. Jesus promised, "Seek, and you shall find."[1] If Anthony Junior continues to seek, he will find. It may not be in the Catholic Church, but A.J. will likely find glimmers of truth in music, art galleries, nature, the Bible, and ultimately in some kind of community of authentic believers. A.J. is not the only one looking for meaning, but he is brave enough to step away from the familiar and start sincere pilgrimage.

Tony tells his son, "Even if God is dead, you're still gonna kiss His ass." But his questioning of God is not a good reason for A.J. to be grounded, punished, or coerced. It is time to be honest, read together, pray together, and acknowledge the divine. Matt Bonpensiero, Pussy's son who offers A.J.

counsel, is correct. Hopelessness of life will lead to insanity, like Nietzsche who wound up talking to his horse. Questions for meaning will lead to answers. What sounds like the cry of a heretic ("What are you yelling at me for? Even Grandma says the world has no purpose.") is really the groan of a mystic in search of truth.

Everyone desires confirmation and seeks a sense of belonging. Christopher finds his place by pledging his full allegiance to Tony and laying down his dreams of Tinseltown. He, like all of us, wants to be verified and accepted, but in a morally blurry postmodern world, this is hard to do; no one knows what to think or believe. Things are shifting too fast. Nothing is stable. There must be a constant to anchor to. There must be something sturdier than our relativistic culture we can take root in, something unmovable. Eternal. Constant. God declares in Scripture, "I the LORD do not change."[2] And again, "Every good and perfect gift is from above, coming down from the Father of the heavenly lights, who does not change like shifting shadows."[3] Will A.J.'s journey lead him to the God "who does not change like shifting shadows" or will he take another path at the crossroads and perpetuate his search for meaning and purpose in life?

CONFESSION

"For a good confession three things are necessary: an examination of conscience, sorrow, and a determination to avoid sin."[4]
—St. Alphonsus Liguori

CHAPTER 6

These days, confession is everywhere. Daytime talk show hosts exploit man's depravity by broadcasting it everyday on every major television network, and top magazines sell it as news and entertainment. The holy discipline that devout Christians have practiced for centuries has been replaced with braggadocios tales of man's selfish exploits because the world has forgotten the proper context for confession and that only authentic confession produces change. Transformation occurs when the stories of our lives are exposed and honestly articulated to a God who listens and responds with forgiveness.

We live in fear of isolation, wearing masks to hide our flaws. Our deep desire is to be truly loved for who we are, and we are all searching for a context to make ourselves known. But instead of allowing the eyes of God to explore the landscape of our sometimes dark souls and illuminate the real-life drama of sin and redemption that is performed within us all, we run to the television or newsstand hoping the vulnerability of another will take the place of our own, and one more day passes without confession, without release. The fear grows within us that no one will ever really know us, and thus we will never know true love. But in confession, we connect with both God and man.

As mankind searches for true love and acceptance, the vulnerability required to move into confession is feared. In pain, a young man dying of AIDS longs for that kind of connection in a hospital bed, shaking with fear of his certain fate. God, to him, is a taskmaster who punishes sin, someone to be feared. A nurse offers this man a treatment called therapeutic touch in a last-ditch effort to relieve his pain. He instantly relaxes; his muscles and aches go numb as his eyes roll back in his head. He thanks the nurse for his newfound peace, saying, "You will never know what you just did for me. I have experienced unconditional love." Soon after this, the man dies. The nurse has given a gift to a weak man who could not give anything back. She knew who he was and felt his sin and pain and embraced him. True love is not a contract that requires something in return. It gives freely and without reserve.

Tony has examined his conscience and experienced sorrow, but remains unconvinced of his need to be penitent and avoid sin. He has walled in his guilt and hides it from everyone, releasing only the overflow to Dr. Melfi and attempting to hide the vast pool of pain and guilt that torments him. Therefore, according to Liguori, Tony is unfit for good confession. He chooses to disguise his sin with secrets and lies, never experiencing the release that comes from true confession. Tony's unspoken thoughts and deeds are buried deep, hidden in the dark.

Jesus said to His disciples: "There is nothing concealed that will not be disclosed, or hidden that will not be made known."[5] Secrets are eventually discovered; they crawl out of the darkness in search for the light. They become a burden, a volatile liability that damages the body and wounds the spirit. Like Tony's dear friend-turned-FBI-witness, Pussy, whose secret betrayal brought on psychosomatic back pain, most people are dying on the inside, always wondering if anyone would love them if they really knew the truth.

Tony is overtaken by this fear as well. He conceals a part of who he is from almost everyone in his life out of fear that they may withdraw from him. He hides mistresses from his family. His criminal activity from his children. His therapy from his associates. And his fears and insecurities from almost everyone. These lies have set fire to his soul and have ignited feelings of extreme anxiety and depression. His lies betray him—the truth is found in the scents he carries home and the guilt in his eyes. He cannot hide reality from his wife, children, and colleagues. And his panic attacks are proving he can no longer hide it from himself.

The same lies and pretenses continually destroy the trust and love native to this family. In the brief moments of their true confession, though, there is a renewed hope. During a long car trip Meadow asks her father The Big Question: "Are you in the mafia?" Tony gasps for air; a lifetime of fear projects into this singular moment. When Tony admits the truth, acknowledging what is already known, it is like a dam that has been broken. There is great relief. Meadow glows in the light of the truth, embracing a new relationship of openness with her father. And it doesn't stop there; she opens her life, sharing a personal story of drug use to her father. She says, "We have that kind of relationship, right?" What kind of relationship is she speaking of, and why has this confirmation of her father's criminal activities produced such joy within her? It is the honesty of this new relationship. The love that

is shared is no longer built on a lie. It is real and unconditional. This is the kind of love God has for His creation, a
perfect love that "drives out fear."[6]

During the same trip with his daughter to visit a prospective
university, Tony reads a quote that is posted ominously on a
sign above an office door: "No man can wear one face to
himself and another to the multitude without finally getting
bewildered as to which may be true." Tony has lost himself.
The artificial has become so familiar that he has forgotten
the real. It's time to step out of the dark and reach out to
someone who may serve as a friend and guide. This might be
his bride, a captain, or his priest. The New Testament says,
"Confess your sins to each other and pray for each other so
that you may be healed. The prayer of a righteous man is
powerful and effective."[7] Dietrich Bonhoeffer agreed and
wrote, "As long as I am by myself in the confession of my sins
everything remains in the dark, but in the presence of a
brother the sin has to be brought to light."[8] Real confession
requires a reliance on someone else, an acknowledgement
that we cannot make it on our own. Will Tony attempt to
expose his hidden life and find release, taking the first step
toward God and redemption by acknowledging and confessing the true self?

Tony's true self is trying to be revealed, and is forcing itself to
the surface. But, "the false self is deeply entrenched. You can
change your name, your address, religion, country, and
clothes. But as long as you don't ask it to change, the false self
simply adjusts to the new environment," said Father Thomas

Keating. "For example, instead of drinking your friends under the table as a significant sign of self-esteem and worth, you enter a monastery as I did. Fasting the monks under the table could become your new path to glory. In that case, what would have changed? Nothing."[9] Tony's problems are deeper than his circumstances. If you move the Soprano family to a beach community in Florida, Tony will still be Tony, a man owned by the secrets of his past, present, and future, a man in need of confession who waits in fear of judgment.

"If we confess our sins, he is faithful and just and will forgive us our sins and purify us from all unrighteousness."[10] —1 John 1:9

WHERE THE FIRE NEVER GOES OUT

C.S. Lewis offers counsel to guide the discussion of eternal damnation: "In all discussions of Hell we should keep steadily before our eyes the possible damnation not of our enemies, nor our friends ... but of ourselves."[11]

The place of fiery torment, spoken of in the Bible as the prison for the damned, is angst to the Soprano clan who fear it may be their eternal home. Tony feels differently though, saying for him there is nothing to fear. He believes hell is for the "worst people, the twisted and demented psychos who kill people for pleasure, the degenerate bastards who molest and torture little kids and kill babies, the Hitlers, the Paul Potts. Those are the evil fucks that deserve to die." He doesn't even mention the mafia. He claims he does not fit the criteria. However, Carmela sees things differently. She confronts Tony and says, "The only difference between you and me is you're going to hell when you die."

David Hume said, "Heaven and hell suppose two distinct species of men, the good and the bad. But the greatest part of mankind float betwixt vice and virtue."[12] Hell is not a place for the bad people. As Scripture says, "All people have sinned and fall short of the glory of God."[13] It is a place of separation from the divine, exile from all that is good. Hell is a place where one who has rejected forgiveness is left to eternally reap the consequences of his sin. This one-dimensional existence is a prison overflowing with one's own anger, resentment, selfishness, and loneliness. The grace available on earth in connection with the Creator is absent.

Consider Christopher lying wounded in a hospital bed dying from a gunshot wound. In a flurry of activity, the doctors begin to respond to heart failure. They're too late. Christopher is dead. During the next few minutes Christopher has a vision of hell. In an act of mercy he is spared and wakes to tell of his journey. Christopher claims he "crossed over to the other side." He describes hell as an Irish bar where it's St. Patrick's Day every day. The men he had killed are there. His father is there. And Christopher warns Tony and Paulie about the constant torment, saying in hell his father was murdered in a different way every night. Tony reduces Christopher's vision to a morphine trip, but Paulie sees it differently.

CHAPTER 6

Paulie is tormented by thoughts of his uncertain eternity. He awakes to visions and nightmares and at one point jumps violently out of bed screaming, "They're dragging me to hell!" He sought guidance from a psychic and then from his priest, but to no avail. Now Paulie is alone and afraid and forced to seek justification and answers in places unknown. Historically, both priests and pastors have abused the concept of hell. Clergy would manipulate their congregations through fear and coerce them into "a life of faith." This kind of faith lacks real spiritual vitality and leaves the so-called faithful empty-handed and still searching for a loving God. In reaction to this abuse of power one might lose sight of real eternal consequences. Paulie is unable to resolve the actuality of his eternal damnation. He believes in God, heaven, and hell and has even tabulated his time in purgatory based on the number of his venial and mortal sins. But hell is a place of pain that is difficult to grasp in human understanding. At three o' clock in the morning, nothing is more real.

Unlike Paulie, Tony won't admit his fears. He wonders and has doubts about eternity and God and heaven and hell. He even asks Pussy, "Do you believe in God?" But when confronted by Dr. Melfi about the eternal consequences of his business, Tony responds, "We're soldiers. We follow codes. Soldiers don't go to hell. It's war." He sees himself as innocent and therefore safe from the punishment of hell.

No one wants to admit his sin and confess, but there comes a time in everyone's life when the consequences must be faced and eternity acknowledged. If the boss were to acknowledge his deep-seated fear that there may be eternal consequences for his sin, something would have to change. Music critic and contributor to *Times magazine*, Terry Teachout, reminds us, "[Tony] believes in God, as do his friends and colleagues. Indeed, Tony and his friends spent the better part of a recent episode speculating on whether there is a hell—a question of immediate personal relevance, since they are all multiple murderers."[14] Because Tony refuses to acknowledge the possibility of eternal consequences, his unspoken questions of eternity remain unanswered. He keeps them hidden, and there is a sea of doubt and despair about how God sees him and his families.

Jesus said, "If your hand causes you to sin, cut it off. It is better for you to enter life maimed than with two hands to go into hell, where the fire never goes out. And if your foot causes you to sin, cut it off. It is better for you to enter life crippled than to have two feet and be thrown into hell. And if your eye causes you to sin, pluck it out. It is better for you to enter the kingdom of God with one eye than to have two eyes and be thrown into hell, where 'their worm does not die, and the fire is not quenched.' Everyone will be salted with fire."[15] Jesus is not advocating self-mutilation; He is warning people of the devastating consequences of sin and the extreme measures one should take in avoiding it.

Despite the ominous way damnation overshadows religious life, hell is not the focus of Scripture. In fact it is mentioned only about a dozen times in the Bible (as opposed to heaven, which is mentioned 421 times). Instead, the primary focus of

Scripture is love, the story of Christ, a romance about grace and forgiveness. Being separated from that story and that God is hell. It is ultimate condemnation, the ultimate alienation. T.S. Eliot wrote, "Hell is oneself. Hell is alone, the other figures in it, merely projections. There is nothing to escape from and nothing to escape to. One is always alone."[16] For everyone who is in Christ, meaning all who know Him and the inexhaustible forgiveness He brings, there is no condemnation. No alienation. And no fear of hell.

ISOLATION
DUCKS, DELUSIONS, AND DEPRESSION

The world meets Tony Soprano as he sits in a waiting room looking very curiously at a statue of a naked woman, just outside the office of his psychiatrist, Dr. Melfi. She opens her door and asks, "Mr. Soprano?" Tony nods, walks into her office and has a seat. He looks around the room, seemingly bored and uncomfortable, and says nothing. She looks at him and waits. (Very typical of a psychotherapy session.) Here the tension begins: not knowing how to look at a woman, not knowing why he's there, not knowing what to say. The show is born in a tension shrouded by silence; this awkwardness is an incessant reminder of these gangsters' uncertainty and loneliness. Dr. Melfi initiates dialogue and therapy begins.

Tony tells the story of two ducks from Canada that migrated to New Jersey and made their home in the Soprano's pool. The ducks soon mated and had several ducklings. This new family stayed in his pool until the young were able to fly. And one afternoon, as Tony was grilling food for his teenage son's birthday party, the ducks flew away. This chilling sight caused Tony to have a panic attack and pass out. Later, through therapy, Tony realizes his deepest fears of loss and loneliness. He first becomes aware of his feelings as he retells the story of a dream he had the night before to Dr. Melfi.

Tony fidgets with his tie and stares aimlessly around the room. Very awkwardly, he begins to describe his dream. In the dream his bellybutton was a Phillips head screw. As Tony says this he motions to his stomach as if unscrewing something. Then, in the dream, when he was finished unscrewing the screw, his penis fell off. Melfi pauses and raises her brow. Tony continues, "You know, I pick it up and I'm holdin' it and I'm runnin' around looking for the guy who used to work on my Lincoln when I drove Lincolns so he can put it back on. And, you know, I'm holdin' it up and this bird swoops down and grabs it in its beak, and flies off with it." She asks, nonchalantly, "What kind of bird?" He shrugs and replies, "I don't know, a seagull or something.'" "A duck?" With a sudden change of mood Tony replies, "Those goddamn ducks."

Dr. Melfi is curious why these ducks mean so much to Tony. Shaking his head and with tears in his eyes, Tony remembers the joy it was to have those ducks in his pool. He pauses, acknowledging the sorrow of watching them leave, and begins to cry. Dr. Melfi passes the tissues across the table to dry the tears of this conflicted Mafioso. She puts it together and deduces that when the ducks had babies it became a family. This is it. A breakthrough. Tony's great fear is that he will lose his family. He is constantly full of dread, fearing that he will end up alone, isolated.

Not only is the office of a psychiatrist becoming a familiar American institution, but these feelings of loneliness and fears of loss are increasingly prevalent as well. We connect with Tony because we feel lonely too. We question the integrity of those who claim to love us.

In the film, *The Mexican*, James Gandolfini's character (a homosexual hit man) asks Julia Roberts' character a heart-rending question: "If you really love someone when do you come to the place where enough is enough?" The answer is you don't. Real love is unconditional. Most of us fear that if friends and family saw us for who we really are, they would turn their backs and leave. So we perpetuate the charade, always wondering what real love truly is. We long for the kind of love that embraces our flaws and defects unconditionally. Intimate encounters lure us out of our detached world filled with fear and anxiety. But without unconditional love we remain disconnected. Alienated. Alone. Some seek restoration through psychotherapy and medication. Some search for peace in the spiritual and mystical. But the connection is that we all seek it.

Like Tony and those ducks, we all have stories. We all have fears. Maybe this is why millions tune in each week to eavesdrop on Tony's sessions in therapy. Could it be that we all feel so detached from anything and everything greater than ourselves that we, like Tony, need to hear—week after week—Dr. Melfi's advice? Or maybe we all just need someone to talk to?

Tony's feelings of detachment are clearly seen when he violently threatens his Jewish business associate, Sholomo Teittleman, demanding he fulfill his end of the deal and pay up. Sholomo refuses and calls him a monster, a Frankenstein. This sinks deep within Tony, and the weight of such a statement is revealed in his next session with Dr. Melfi. Tony says, almost jokingly, that someone called him a Frankenstein. Melfi asks, "Do you feel like Frankenstein?" She pauses. "A thing ... lacking humanity ... lacking human feelings?" Tony just sits in silence with a sad face staring at the floor. And the scene ends. But as this scene fades, the curtain is lifted on the stage of our own lives.

The drama of our personal struggle to be human despite our monstrosity is mirrored for us in this penetrating scene (as well as many others). Tony's feelings of loneliness and his fear of loss are given a foundation here. His medication and therapy goals are not to experience a change in his lifestyle, but simply to ease the pain and guilt that overwhelms him. He feels like Frankenstein, not fully beast, not fully man, disconnected from everyone in his life. Incapable of empathy, he is dulling his senses to avoid the trauma of his own actions and is losing all sense of love and connectedness in the process. Like Frankenstein, he winds up afraid and alone.

Death, the ultimate separation, looms over this show like a dense fog. In addition to the ever-present mystery of God and eternity, we are plagued by the fear of death and by the manner in which we will all inevitably die. Livia articulates this fear of isolation and separation from the world when she says to A.J., "In the end, you die in your own arms." Alone.

But Tony knows there must be more. He fears the loss of family and is searching for real human connection. Fears of abandonment and rejection paralyze the ultimate male, so he seeks psychiatric treatment. But Tony is standing in his own way. His lifestyle demands that he remain isolated, for in isolation we cease to feel, and this is the only way Tony can brutally kill a man and then go home and sit down to dinner with his family.

But to cease to feel is to stop living. When we allow life circumstances, or our own choices, to harden the essence of true humanity so to dull the pain, we do become like Frankenstein. A monster.

"I wish the Lord would take me now." —Livia Soprano

LIVIA SOPRANO

It's not the competing crime families, the persistent threats of the FBI, the lingering indictments, or even the betrayal of a lifelong friend that torment Tony's earthly existence. It is his mother, Livia Soprano. This vile matriarch of the Soprano family is a forbidding woman and the most destructive monster on a show full of monsters. In the disguise of a typical Italian-American mother, she chooses to terrorize rather than nurture.

From the very beginning of *The Sopranos*, Livia is a miserable and shrill old woman. She complains about everything—from the way Tony prepares meat to be cooked to people calling her at home after dark. She's ungrateful even when she receives gifts and is predictably insincere. This neurotic, manipulative, power-hungry terror lives a life devoid of friendship. Dr. Melfi describes her as a woman with "an almost mystical ability to wreak havoc." She's the kind of woman Billy Joel says would "carelessly cut you and laugh while you're bleeding." Even at her funeral, there is nothing kind to say.

She dismantles the strong persona of all the seemingly dominant men in her life with very crafty passive/aggressive manipulation. Even her husband, Johnny Boy, was no match for her. In one of his sessions Tony confesses to Dr. Melfi, "My dad was tough; he ran his own crew. A guy like that and my mother wore him down to a little nub. He was a squeaky little gerbil when he died."

Livia knows the family business and loves it. When Johnny considered "going legit" she would have no part of it. She wore the pants. She was the boss, and after being reminded of his father's wishes to leave the "business," Tony confronts her, "Everybody thought dad was the ruthless one; but I gotta hand it to you, if you had been born after those feminists, you would have been the real gangster."

Even while she's hidden away at Green Grove, the $4,000 a month retirement community where she occupies a corner suite with a woods view, Livia continues to run the show. Tony's Uncle Junior, the acting boss, does not make any substantial decisions without her consent. He wouldn't dare. This is more than permission; Livia pulls the strings and these boys are her puppets. She even sentences Christopher's friend, Brendan, to death with a simple shrug of her shoulders.

She wields the same power in her family. Livia is a testimony to the supremacy of motherhood. She cannot be shaken despite her repulsive behavior. Her children still love her and desire her support. Her son spends time, energy, and money in hopes that he can give her happiness. But her misery works well for her. She uses the power she has as a mother and abuses her maternal gift. Carmela confronts her about it, "I am a mother too, don't forget. You know the power that you have, and you use it like a pro." Livia responds, "Power? What power? I don't have power. I'm a shut-in." Carmela replies, "You're bigger than life. You are his mother, and I don't think for one second that you don't know what you're doing to him." What was intended as a tool to build her children up, Livia uses to tear them down and control them.

So much for the intimacy between mothers and daughters in the Soprano family; it is non-existent. Tony's two sisters, Barbara and Janice, left New Jersey on the first train out, and as for Carmela, she wouldn't dream of such a bond with her discontent mother-in-law. On Tony and Carmela's wedding day Livia pulled Carmela aside and shattered the new bride's fragile heart, "It was a mistake. Tony will get bored with you."

Obligation is the glue in Livia's relationships; why else would anyone befriend this dejected and spiteful woman? She uses manipulation to bring others closer to her as she seeks to control them, but it drives them away. Tony reaches out because of something more than familial obligation; he loves her.

Yet this feeble one hundred pound woman strikes fear into the heart of her son. As if she stands behind every dark corner, Livia haunts all of Tony's sessions with Dr. Melfi. Tony squirms at the mention of her name or questions of her impact. He resents the therapeutic escape that continues to pass his guilt to Mama Soprano, frequently marching out of Melfi's office in disgust. But Tony always comes back. Social commentator Nancy Friday says, "Blaming mother is just a negative way of clinging to her still."[1]

This is easily seen. It is clear Tony's deepest desire is to be loved by his mother. As a grown man he continues to pander for her approval. He even has a delusional relationship with a beautiful Italian woman whom he desires to be his mother, fantasizing about being breastfed in a picturesque nursery. The mother he dreams of is the anti-Livia, different in every way, beautiful but not sexual, and a skilled listener. A nurturer.

There does not seem to be a nurturing bone in Livia's body. Throughout the entire journey of *The Sopranos*, she is obsessed with infanticide, constantly speaking of the mother from Pennsylvania who shot her three kids and set her house on fire, or news reports of mothers in New York throwing their babies out of windows. She even admits, "Babies are like animals. They're no different than dogs." This fascination creeps into the home.

In a flashback Tony remembers his mother violently threatening to stab a fork through his eye (a scene based on an experience David Chase had as a child with his own mother); and later, while eavesdropping on his parents, Tony hears his mother telling his father she would rather smother Tony and his two other sisters with a pillow than let him take them to Nevada. All this from a woman who says, "I gave my life to my children on a silver platter." This is motherhood. Redefined.

When interrogated by Dr. Melfi about any warm, loving memory he had involving his mother, Tony recalls a time thirty years ago when the entire Soprano family went to the beach. He remembers his family walking along the shore and his father tripping over something and falling down. "We were all laughing," he says. "My mother was laughing."

Dr. Melfi made her point. Tony can't remember a single joyful experience with his mother. It is sad; a lifetime with his mother passed without a single pleasant memory. This is the power of Livia Soprano. She goes to the grave choosing never to affirm a son who desperately desired to know her love. As a result, Tony will spend his days probing his life and relationship for something to fill that void, a love that does not come with conditions and cannot be found under the sun.

ALL IN THE FAMILY

"The LORD God said, 'It is not good for man to be alone.'"
—Genesis 2:18

CHAPTER 7

Everyone in the Soprano families knows they need each other. A daughter needs her mother, a boss needs his captains, a husband needs his wife, and so on. Independence is not a value or an option; it's suicide. This is not a business that promotes individuality; it is a family that requires community and commitment.

A sense of deep belonging and interconnectedness in both of these families anchors lives otherwise plagued with chaos. In "this thing" the boundaries are clear. You are either in or out. A covenant exists here much like the covenant between the Hebrew God and His people, a covenant of loyalty and honor. But there is one unforgivable sin: to get flipped, which means to turn state's evidence and burn the people who love you most. Families are built on a shared purpose, a common identity. The Hebrew people describe it as a corporate personality; they find their identity together. In this family their existence is based on seeking the greater good through fidelity and love. Tony's criminal family also find their identity together in what they simply call "this thing of ours." Neither covenant is to be broken. It is more than a promise; it is a way of life.

Tony knows any family member in isolation is vulnerable. If unprotected by his community, each man becomes an open target. You don't advance in this business by working on your own. Learning comes from the experience and the teaching from the ones further down the road than you. Tony Soprano has his nephew Christopher, a soldier, ride with Paulie, a captain, to learn the ropes of the family business. In this business, a soldier should learn from the captain, and a captain from the boss and consigliere. Maturity requires togetherness.

The same is true at the Soprano home. Everyone sits down to eat a meal together as a family. There is no kids' table. Three generations of Sopranos break bread and share life on a daily basis. This is a sacred time and tardiness is not acceptable. All business is put aside to be together.

Isolation is the great evil on this show. Even Tony, the ruthless leader and family patriarch, deeply fears rejection and ending up alone. How is it that this man, who seems to have it all, lacks the confidence to face challenges that may be around the corner? Because money, pleasure, and success are only temporal and are lost as quickly as they are gained. Riches can be squandered, love can turn to hate, and ill-gotten pleasure is like a caffeine high that is brief, but the crash that follows sticks with you long after the burst of energy. The approval of man is conditional at best. There must be something more, something spiritual, a tie that truly binds, a chord that cannot be severed.

The togetherness of the Soprano families has captivated viewers. The most appealing part of the mafia is participation in this covenant family. For a generation of broken homes and distant families, the concept of a loving and faithful community sounds too good to be true. People want connection, something they can attach to and be a part of. This does not mean family life is easy. Real families should not lack tension and discord. Peace is a lousy goal. When one tries to avoid all conflict, he will inevitably live in turmoil. Disagreement is an essential ingredient to every family, so resolution and compromise must be learned with children and the capos. When strife surfaces a man requests a sit down where the boss of the family will see that things are resolved. Families function well when there is a structure to deal with the conflict that is inevitable.

Safety lies in truly knowing one another, in finding a place to be real. These men seek and long for that protected space. Love is expressed freely in the criminal family. These men kiss one another more often than newlyweds. But revealing their Achilles' heel, their vulnerability, to each other seems unimaginable. Acknowledging Tony's weekly therapy sessions and their desire to be real, Silvio says, "Look, this thing of ours, the way it's going, it'd be better if we could admit to each other these are painful, stressful times. But it'll never fucking happen." These men love one another, but find it impossible to own up to their weakness and humanity, despite the fact it glares everyone in the face, including themselves.

Being noticed, cared for, and respected, that is family. It happens as the families gather around the table, barbecue pit, billiards, and sometimes a coffin. It grounds their existence and calls them to be something better than they are. That is community.

PSYCHOLOGY
TOMATO SAUCE FOR YOUR ASS

The Sopranos is not great simply because it is a mafia story. The strength and power of this criminal underworld are only appealing because its tender underbelly is exposed weekly in the postmodern womblike confines of Dr. Melfi's office. The words, "We are soldiers," roll off Tony's tongue regularly. And in this battle for the spoils of capitalism, the general is deeply wounded.

During one session Tony confesses honestly, "Sometimes I resent you making me a victim, that's all." Of course no one can make anyone a victim. But Melfi offers hyperbolic excuses such as, "Your parents made it impossible for you to experience joy." Impossible? We have seen Tony at the height of ecstasy. He is not incapable. He simply needs a guide, a compass pointing to something else. The self-focused psycho-nonsense of Dr. Melfi is far from a real cure. James Gandolfini has said that David Chase defined *The Sopranos* as a show about "people who lie to themselves, as we all do. Lying to ourselves on a daily basis and the mess it creates."[1] Does Tony truly want to own up to his unlawful lifestyle and poor choices? If someone besides his wife would speak truth into his life, he might begin to listen. For now he continues to live in the drivel, blaming everyone from his parents to his wife.

Tony spits in the face of danger and then cowers in the presence of a helpless old woman. He survives an assassination attempt, and then hyperventilates at the realization that his daughter is dating an African-American. Tony has lived out a lifetime of bad decisions; he has played out his vain imagination and the consequences are coming home to haunt him. He cannot handle the truth, and is searching for a diversion to distract him from the ugly reality of his criminal life.

Psychotherapy and Tony's professional priestess, Dr. Melfi, try to avoid the ruin that results from bad choices. Dr. Melfi says, "With today's pharmacology no one should have to suffer from feelings of pain and depression." No one? Not even the guilty? Should adulterers have to live with the pain of their betrayal and malice? Should murderers have to face the visions of the men they've killed and the ways they've killed them? Absolutely. Everyone should feel the pain of his own decisions. It's what makes people become better. It brings maturity and leads the way out of selfishness.

Pharmacology primarily helps to hide the reality. It helps to avoid the disgusting truth in an inner world that is already buried. When discussing the medication prescribed by Dr. Melfi, Tony admits, "On this shit I don't feel nothin'. I'm dead, empty." He attempts to prop up his fallen world with each pill he consumes. Lack of repentance is taking its toll. Prozac only serves as an aid. "I find I have to be the sad clown, laughing on the outside, crying on the inside," is how Tony puts it. Medication makes it easier to paint the face and fake the laugh, but the cry quickly turns into a sob because the pills provide only a temporary fix. There is still no lasting hope.

If Prozac fails to divert the anxiety of Tony's criminally selfish life, there remains a toolbox full of other therapeutic escapes. Lithium. Xanax. Doctors can make this a medical problem and diagnose it as a disease, or people can begin to see the emptiness found in an overstocked medicine cabinet and begin the search for something more.

Dr. Melfi insists that Tony suffers from a medical problem. It's the only way she can justify treating him, "If he had a pituitary tumor would I stop him from seeing me?" Comparing Tony's guilt-driven panic to a tumor is absurd, but his psychiatrist desperately tries to make his issues medical ones. She says she feels obligated to work with Tony. But Dr. Melfi's ex-husband is not fooled by this defense. He assails her for rationalizing her relationship with Tony Soprano in psychological terms and trenchantly observes that ultimately it's a question of good and evil, and Tony Soprano is evil. The truth is that Tony is sick, but this sickness is not merely psychological—it is spiritual. It's about eternal decisions of right and wrong. It's time someone begins treating the problem and not the symptoms. It's time for change.

The actual causes of his anxiety are not hard to uncover. Carmela is quick to point them out, "Maybe you should explore your own behavior. Maybe you pass out because you're guilty over something."

Carmela is right. People panic when they realize they're guilty, and people are guilty because they've sinned. This fact cannot be ignored. To understand sin we must return to the first page of the story of mankind. Adam and Eve violated God's order when they tried to take control. The fruit they ate promised knowledge that would make them like God. They wanted a spot in the driver's seat, to become the foreman of paradise, the CEO of the garden. It was all about control. Things haven't changed much.

Tony sets his goals for life and therapy a bit high. He says, "I wanna be in total control." He cannot handle the reality that chaos reigns in a crime family where rules should bring order. When told that possessing total control is not possible, he responds with one word: "Bullshit." The stumbling block for our own spiritual progress has not changed. People want to be God, not man, creator instead of creation. Unless man is willing to acknowledge the place he occupies in this universe, life will be a series of panic attacks and prescriptions. It is natural for man to seize the illusion of control, but a contemplative spiritual walk will dethrone this self-absorbed quest for power. Only then will panic be replaced with peace; the knowledge that it is better to have the Creator of heaven and earth in control than any of His creations brings definitive freedom.

Although Dr. Melfi is careful not to judge or even question the possibility that the life Tony has chosen could have created this mess, in a heated session she finally hints toward personal responsibility. She later cries to her therapist, "I'm living in a moral never-never land with this patient. Not wanting to judge, but to treat. But now I've judged. I took a position, goddamn it, and I'm scared."

Never is the tension between responsibility and psychobabble seen more clearly than when Anthony Junior is diagnosed with ADD after stealing sacramental wine from the church and getting drunk at his Catholic school. His behavior seems normal to this family, but in the new millennium people don't deal with or prevent deviant behavior by training their children. They diagnose and psychoanalyze. Tony knows all too well this is not a disease; it is a choice. "Maybe I don't want to admit there is something wrong with my kid, but it all sounds like bullshit to me," he says. The desire to pass the buck for A.J. is tempting. "If he's got this thing, we'll deal with it. If he had polio we would deal with that, so that's what we are gonna do. Pick up the pieces and go on from there," he says. At one point Tony even suggests that his mafia involvement must be genetic, "You're born to this shit. You are what you are." But if this is true, how have Pussy's kids risen above it all and become scholars and moral citizens?

These answers are not easy to find in the church or in popular spirituality literature like *Chicken Soup for the Soul,* or the Italian version, *Tomato Sauce for your Ass,* which is recommended by Tony. The reality is that most philosophies of life are fatally flawed by their disregard of the blemished state of man. Mankind is typically viewed as either totally good or totally bad. This cannot be true. Blaise Pascal clarifies the issue, saying, "I condemn equally those who choose to praise man, those who choose to condemn him, and those who choose to divert themselves; and I can only approve of those who seek with groans."[2] In this show there are characters who occupy all of these spaces. Charmaine Bucco and others see Tony as entirely bad. Carmela sees both and longs to redeem the good. Dr. Melfi ignores reality and places false blame while offering an escape from the truth (i.e. Prozac). Tony is seeking with groans.

Professional help is not helping. Tony pays $175 per hour for a safe place to be authentic with no lasting results. Livia has a low view of psychotherapy, calling it crazy. "It's all non-sense," she says. "It's nothing but a racket for the Jews." She says it's "what people do when they are looking for somebody to blame for their life." Carmela is also skeptical. She vents her frustration during their first marital session with Dr. Melfi. She speaks plainly when asked about her dissatisfaction. Dr. Melfi asks about her incapacity to change Tony. Carmela replies, "I was referring to your inability to help him." After all, Tony has been seeing her for three years and he is still passing out. With all that money, they could have added a new wing on the house.

At one point, Dr. Melfi does refuse to see Tony, but she feels guilty about it. She has a dream that Tony dies from a panic attack while driving. It's her fault, like the client who com-

mitted suicide—because she wasn't there to help. She is prepared to take responsibility, but still refusing to point to
where the blame truly belongs. Carmela sees this and points
out the fatal flaw saying, "Psychology doesn't address the
soul, that's something else. But this is a start." Her greatest
hope is that Tony's therapy opens the door to real change,
change that deals with the soul. That is the ultimate question for Tony. Will he acknowledge the bankruptcy of the
psychological blame game, take responsibility for a life of
selfish ambition, and begin seeking spiritual healing? Or will
he spend his days in therapy, dancing around the real issues?

DR. MELFI

Dr. Jennifer Melfi lives in an impossible predicament,
attempting to heal Tony Soprano and other misguided
patients without possessing a true sense of the illness in her
own life. She sits in a place of perceived power but, like Tony,
finds herself weak and bankrupt. When she glances at her
desk calendar and sees the initials "TS," she quickly retreats
to her liquor cabinet. But drinking a glass of bourbon as fore-
play to her hour-long sit-down with the mob boss is only the
beginning of Dr. Melfi's ethical dilemmas.

She tiptoes carefully through the minefield of Tony's criminal activities, choosing to avoid language with any moral
fiber. Melfi may not have all the facts, but the business of
murder, extortion, loan sharking, and the like is coming
clearly into focus. She promises never to judge a patient's

behavior, and this fear of becoming judgmental stifles any potential she has to speak truth and healing into Tony's life. The possibility of transformation is dissolved by her silence.

Dr. Melfi has abandoned all ethical predicate by treating the incurable patient and choosing to ignore the reality that his life needs more than psychotherapy; it needs justice, which invokes a judgment of right and wrong. Instead of addressing the real issues of Tony's life, Dr. Melfi chooses to teach Tony better coping skills. She seems to believe that righting this man will restore her hope in mankind and herself. But offering self-help to Tony Soprano only makes him a more successful gangster, and this is immoral. She is aware of the tension. On one hand she does not want to be dragged into the moral quicksand that is Tony's life, and on the other she longs to see him healed.

Despite meager attempts on both of their parts to end this relationship, Dr. Melfi continues to see Tony; something has bound these two together. She refuses to let him go. Dr. Melfi is drawn to power like a moth to light. Tony possesses immense clout and an aura of mystery. The good doctor admires it and is in awe of this intangible quality that defines her patient. Melfi typifies American culture, in which many women are drawn to powerful men. She finds safety in knowing Tony Soprano. Every week they trudge through Tony's problems as the sexual tensions grow. In a strange dance, they volley affection, despair, and love back and forth. The charade continues, absent of any real signs of hope.

One night after work, Dr. Melfi falls victim to a rapist who waits for her in a dark parking garage. She is brutally forced to have sex in a concrete stairwell. She emerges alive but severely wounded. Left with a bloody, swollen face and a distended leg, the illusion of safety is destroyed. The hope of justice fades when this violent sexual offender is released on a technicality, free to return to work at a burger joint around the corner, and free to repeat these violent acts against someone else, possibly even a child. The world is not right. Nothing is fair or just. Nevertheless, Dr. Melfi now has the opportunity to see justice rendered. With a carefully-placed phrase Tony would act, and this burger-flipping pervert would never endanger anyone again. He would never even be seen again. Instead Melfi chooses to hold her tongue. Though it feels good to have life and death hinge on her words, the power to take a man's life with a whisper, she chooses to hold her tongue.

She is playing with fire, struggling to maintain a semblance of her professional ethics but longing for the freedom of Tony Soprano to say what she wants to say and do what she longs to do. When she drinks, Melfi loses her inhibitions and lives like Tony. When annoyed by a woman smoking in a restaurant, she orders her to "put out the fucking cigarette." The woman defies her, and she lunges at her and is expelled from the premises. Deep down, Jennifer Melfi is a lot like Tony, and this both excites and scares her.

Dr. Melfi has the potential to connect with Tony on a deep level. As a fellow journeyer, she could be a tremendous help to him, choosing through honesty and confession to speak truth and restoration into his self-defined meaningless life. She rightfully probes the deep issues, uncovering the trash and treasures that lie far below the surface of Tony's skin, yet hides any glimpse of her own humanity. If Dr. Melfi came to grips with her own wantonness, she could possibly provide healing insight to Tony and witness real change occur in his life and in the life of his families. Melfi also stands in need of forgiveness, love, and peace that will only be found on a spiritual journey, not in a prescription.

In journeying through the pain and healing that she has experienced, Melfi could offer Tony a true story of hope and affirmation that he is not alone in a world of despair; a fellow pilgrim could comfort him. Instead she chooses to sit and diagnose and prescribe, disconnected from her own life and experience. She could descend her professional pedestal and acknowledge their shared disappointment in life, blessing Tony as a peer on a common path. But her life remains closed off to Tony, and to herself. Dr. Melfi attempts to reassemble the broken pieces of Tony's shattered life while being overwhelmed by the rubble of her own. To help Tony she would have to bring her own issues to light, digging deep within to excavate her own problems. This would mean abandoning the false façade that hides her real life and revealing the truth. Without the curtain coming down, she will be incapable of rendering guidance to Tony in the midst of his brokenness. There will be no helpful connection. No redeeming therapy. The missing link in the process of healing is her accurate understanding of the healing she needs. Dr. Melfi could be a wounded healer, healing out of pain. Instead, she is only wounded.

While Dr. Melfi tries to help Tony grapple with the symptoms of stress, anxiety, and depression, the deeper questions of life are left unanswered. Father Thomas Keating stated these questions well, saying, "All the questions that are fundamental to human happiness arise when we ask ourselves this excruciating question: Where am I? Where am I in relation to God, to myself, and to others?"[3] Keating defines these as the basic questions of human life. Tony is lost. He, along with his therapist, is searching to find where he is. But neither Tony nor Dr. Melfi has faced this central question. They are searching for happiness and contentment in all the wrong places. It is the blind leading the blind, falling into one therapeutic ditch after another.

There has to be counsel that deals with right and wrong, something that works on the heart and addresses the soul. No psychiatrist is prepared to be a spiritual director, but this is the only place Tony goes to find healing. Melfi speaks only in jargon, not in the exchange of stories. She builds a weak bridge of psychological nonsense and prescriptions over the rushing waters of sin and instructs Tony to take a step of faith. When Tony tries to cross from death to life over this feeble structure, he falls and is continually swept away by the unconfessed sin. Tony wants to see a picture of a life changed or at least a life changing, but hope is absent when the stories of deliverance are left untold. Therapy only leads to more therapy, an increased dosage instead of increased stability.

Tony quickly begins to see this and realizes that the endless merry-go-round of prescriptions offers no real results. Dr. Melfi asks, "Are you still taking the lithium?" He replies, "Lithium. Prozac. When's it gonna end?"

THE LORD TONY ALMIGHTY

Power. It is the forbidden fruit, the lust of mankind, the ultimate aphrodisiac, and the alluring quality that makes a balding, overweight, inconsiderate suburban father an international sex symbol. Tony Soprano draws women and men to himself because he seems to possess a nearly ultimate authority, some kind of inexplicable might.

In the origins of humanity, man thrust himself into a quest for power and control because of his rebellious desire to be like God. That search has never ended and the ultimate goal of attaining absolute power continues to elude mankind. Tony wants complete control and total dominion over his families and circumstances, and like everyone else he struggles to define his own existence and govern his own destiny. The constant predicament of humanity—how to be godlike—is the inability to write the story, to define the roles, to set the perimeters, to be and act as God. And it is with this predicament that Tony wages war.

Rene Descartes, the father of modern psychology, spurred on the ambition of modern man with the theory that the universe could be understood, that all things are knowable. Ever since Descartes uttered the eventual mantra of modernity, "Cognito ergo sum," translated, "I think, therefore I am," the world has pursued knowledge at all costs. The rationale goes, "I know that I exist because my eight-pound brain tells me this is true," and society has leapt to the conclusion that "knowledge is power." It is more than a jingle on Saturday morning cartoons (following "conjunction junction, what's your function?"). It is a way of life. People embrace this concept because it promises that all things are knowable, that through reason one can understand all of life and God; "Cognito ergo sum" apparently dissolves the mystery.

Science became the new path to peace, happiness, and contentment—in short, power. The scientific theory rose to a place of unprecedented acceptance and soon after crumbled under the pressure. The panacea proved fallible. Science was unable to extract absolute truth from our chaotic world. Even in a vacuum results vary, facts surface at random. Knowledge is deceptive and it changes like the wind. This quest for absolute knowledge is failing, and has modernity against the ropes. The modern world has been built upon a foundation of absolute knowledge, and the world is learning there is so much more to the universe. There is more unknowable than knowable.

The walls of modernity have fallen, but in some sectors men are reassembling the stones in hopes that command of the universe can still be obtained. In laboratories across the globe, men are attempting to become godlike and do the undoable: create life through the cloning and tampering of genetic codes. C.S Lewis offered counsel to mankind if this day ever came, saying, "In reality, of course, if any one age really attains, by eugenics and scientific education, the power to make its descendants what it pleases, all men who live after it are the patients of that power. They are weaker, not stronger: for though we may have put wonderful machines in their hands we have preordained how they are to use them."[4] One of the great mysteries of life is humanity's freedom to choose. Genetic tampering is an effort to limit man's choices, thus changing the very nature of man.

Humanity is not capable of wielding these godlike powers judiciously. We are not even willing to share the resources of the earth, such as clean water and food. How can the same planet be expected to wield the power of creation with wisdom and care? It cannot. We should accept the shackles of humanity and act on what we're able to influence. Instead, we seek the unreachable, and long to know the unknowable.

John Rafferty writes about God from a place of disbelief and skepticism: "What do you call an all-powerful, jealous, and terrible being who is beyond ordinary human concepts of morality and ethics, who demands absolute loyalty and obedience, who takes life, destroys fortune, and dispenses rewards and punishments for reasons and according to rules known only to himself? You might call him God. HBO calls him Tony Soprano."[5] Truly, *The Sopranos* creates the illusion Tony is God in his own world, an almighty being, omnipotent and indestructible.

Although Tony is not the Messiah, this flawed fictional hero does wield tremendous power, and in his family structure there is the illusion he is sovereign and over all. In reality, though, Tony cannot even manage control over his own psyche, and his physical body continues to send him poignant reminders of his very tangible humanity. Instead of seeking complete control, Tony should seek self-control. The Bible describes self-control as the ability, through the divine Spirit of God, to control one's own evil impulses. John Piper writes, "The very concept of 'self-control' implies a battle between a divided self. It implies that our 'self' produces desires we should not satisfy but instead 'control.' We should 'deny ourselves' and 'take up our cross daily,' Jesus says, and follow him (Luke 9:23). Daily our 'self' produces desires that should be 'denied' or 'controlled.'"[6] Tony must heed Piper's biblical advice or self-destruct. He must recognize his inability to govern his universe and submit to the Spirit of his benevolent Creator. For now he ignores the teachings of Christ and, like Solomon, denies himself nothing his heart desires.

These evil impulses are the source of Tony's pain and frustration. He is in a constant struggle for control. Control of the business. Control of his family. Control of himself. He wages war against all of these things in hope of somehow gaining control, but control is not an option. It's a myth. The idea that we are in control, that it is us who rule the world, is only a fairytale. It is God who runs the show, the Creator who rules His creation. Yet Tony believes himself to be Lord Almighty. This is a deep pit of foolishness many fall into. This was humanity's mistake at the dawn of time. Adam and

Eve wanted to be like God, to be in control. So they were eager to believe the serpent's lie when he told them, "When you eat of [the Tree of the Knowledge of Good and Evil] your eyes will be opened, and you will be like God."[7] They ate of the tree, but did not become like God. Instead, they felt shame and hid from their Creator. They gained humiliation, not control. Could this be where Tony will end up? Ashamed of his rebellion, hiding from his Lord, humiliated? Or will he be repentant? One can only hope. Tony desperately needs to come to a place of humility, accepting the will of a higher power and placing his life in God's hands.

His criminal family is on the brink of complete chaos. Paulie is on the brink of betrayal, an act that could mean war with the New York families. His namesake is not welcome at his Catholic school, and his panic-ridden future seems uncertain. The most powerful man in New Jersey is actually powerless.

THE MEN
IN JOGGING SUITS AND SEE-THROUGH SOCKS

CORRADO "JUNIOR" SOPRANO

Corrado "Junior" Soprano's quiet demeanor, coupled with his soft round face and oversized black-rimmed glasses make him a handsome and amiable-looking old man. He's Tony's biological (and professional) uncle, Johnny Boy's older brother. Junior's been mobbed up since the 1940s, an old school gangster. Yet despite the lifetime he's had in the family business, Junior is unprepared to take the reigns and lead the family. Unable to make executive decisions alone, he is either enticed by Mikey Palmice, his annoying and impulsive consigliere, or manipulated into action by his sister-in-law, the dreaded Livia. This liability leaves Junior insecure, always desiring to prove himself as a leader, which he is clearly not.

This same timidity has affected his family situation as well. In his golden years, Junior is without a wife and children. The heirs of his brother, Johnny, are his only family. Despite the apparent drama, it is clear he and Tony love one another.

CHAPTER 9

Tony thinks of him as a good guy, just old and cranky. You can be sure, Junior dreams of a family to call his own, but in both of his families, his sibling overshadows him.

Junior has struggled to be his own man and be respected, but he's passed up for Tony. His nephew has earned the respect of his peers, and despite the fact Junior is given the boss's title, everyone knows Tony calls the shots. This is for good reason. Junior is not the wisest wise guy around. He makes bad choices; he's sloppy on the field. The most significant move he makes as boss is to attempt to kill Tony. For the most dangerous hit he ever orders, he uses some street kids who fail. Junior is now in jeopardy, and though he lives, his crew is mowed down one by one by Tony's loyal soldiers.

Living has been difficult for Corrado Soprano, but he fears death most of all. He is diagnosed with cancer and thinks death looms over him because two other friends have already passed on, and superstition says death comes in threes. This unpredictable old man is the wild card. What will his jealousy of Tony force him to do if left unchecked? Will the reality of his own mortality lead him to faith in God and love of family? He realizes his house is not in order, and he is not prepared to meet his Maker.

Junior's cancer throws him into a tailspin but still has not brought about deep spiritual pursuit. He avoids funerals and any God-talk. But he does believe. Gazing at a prayer card after a funeral he remembers and attempts to understand: "When I was a kid I always used to wonder why no one collected prayer cards like they collect baseball cards. Thousands of bucks for Honus Wagner and jack shit for Jesus."

But spiritual things have been secondary to the business. When deciding to kill long-time gangster Little Pussy (not Tony's soldier, Big Pussy), Junior selects Vesuvio's as the location for the attack. However, Artie Bucco, Tony's childhood friend, owns and operates Vesuvio's. If some mobster gets murdered in his restaurant it'll ruin his business. Tony has to intervene. But this deflates Junior's pride and he lets loose: "You may run North Jersey, but you don't run your Uncle Junior."

Things could go either way with Uncle Jun. He could end his days honoring Tony or he could go down swinging.

CHRISTOPHER MOLTISANTI

"There was a time in my life when being with the Tony Soprano crew was all I ever dreamed of." —Christopher Moltisanti

A sense of youthful exuberance makes Tony's nephew, Christopher Moltisanti, at once very attractive and equally appalling. In his black suit, combed back dark wavy hair, and elongated forehead, he looks the part of a genuine gangster. He went from being a whining kid who complained about stomachaches and misquoted *The Godfather* to a respected "made" man committed to the family. He is still just a boy in this business, but he's quickly moving up in the ranks. He's working his way up the corporate ladder, Mafioso style. Making mistakes. Saving the day.

Christopher's father, Dickie, was a mentor to Tony. Dickie, also Carmela's cousin, was gunned down in a pizza joint when Christopher was a kid. Since then young Christopher has become Tony's project, an adopted nephew. This bond explains his endless patience with the wannabe gangster.

Although it's sometimes hard to see, Christopher respects the family business. When asked by his friend, Brendan, for help on hitting another truck loaded with Italian suits (a job forbidden by the powers that be), he declines. He questions the purpose of criminal community without submission and obedience, "Why be in a crew? Why be a gangster?" Christopher realizes the foolishness of a life in organized crime without organization. There are no lone rangers on the streets of New Jersey, and he knows it. To go it alone in this business would be suicide.

The New York Times says, "Christopher is a soldier of the MTV generation."[1] He is lost in a complex world of moral relativism, and like his postmodern contemporaries, he is overwhelmed and confused. Day after day lines are blurring and bleeding into one another. Roles are shifting. Things are changing. Even in the mob, nobody knows what's what. To escape this reality void of boundaries and a life of sin and a meaningless existence, Christopher turns to drugs, a vice looked down upon in his criminal profession. Like his Uncle

Tony, Christopher is searching for a diversion and turns to mind-altering chemicals to mask the truth. The boss takes his meds by mouth. Christopher takes his up his nose.

Christopher drives a $60,000 Lexus, is engaged to a beautiful woman who believes in him, and is living out his dream of being in the Tony Soprano crew. Yet he remains drawn to drugs to cover his frustration with life. In his first near-death experience, a mock execution by two Czech mobsters, he leaves the hospital in search of cocaine. He tells Tony of his struggle to grapple with these issues explaining, "It's like just the fuckin' regular-ness of life is too fucking hard for me or something." But he should heed the advice he once gave Meadow, "Don't ever say you hate life, that's blasphemy."

He is running from his sin and avoids church and funerals at all cost. After skipping Anthony Junior's confirmation he tells Tony, "I figured with all my sins I don't want the church caving in on anyone." He makes it to the funeral of Tony's mother, but is hopped up on drugs. The first man he murdered, Emil, whom he mockingly calls E-mail, haunts him day and night. After putting a moon roof in the back of his head with a small caliber handgun, Christopher has to come to grips with the fact that he is now a killer. He quickly discovers there is nothing glamorous about taking someone's life.

Christopher loves Tony and the gangster life, but his real goal is fame. It doesn't matter if it comes from a life of crime or from writing mob stories for Hollywood. It just has to come. Christopher thinks his day in the spotlight has come when pending indictments are leaked to the press. To his despair, his name is not mentioned by television reporters, and it is clear that his disappointment will be acted out. When Tony asks Christopher to pick up some sfogliatella, cannolis, and other pastries at Russo's Bakery for the crew at the Bada Bing, he is overtaken by his ambition to establish his name. After waiting impatiently in line, he is skipped by the counter boy who would rather serve a regular customer than an unknown gangster. Christopher's impulsiveness prevails, and in a childlike fit, he forces the customer to leave and shoots the clerk in the foot while stealing the box of pastries.

What is also clear is Tony's love for Christopher. Tony has looked the other way when Christopher made mistakes that could have been punishable by death. Chris is learning from the best. He has paid his dues and will become the man Tony believes he can be. In a moment of self-examination he says to Adriana, "I'm rededicating myself right down the line." He is leaving behind the drugs and rebellion and looking towards marriage, family, and a stable mob income. He is living out the dream of every boy who grows up in New Jersey.

THE BOYS: SILVIO, PAULIE, AND PUSSY

Paulie Walnuts
Paulie is a captain in the Soprano crime family. He is a loyal friend to Tony, a mentor to Christopher, a great earner, and an old-fashioned Italian gangster. He stands tall, about six

feet; is thin but not skinny, and is very muscular with tat-
toos on each well-built arm. He has a great Italian accent,
perfect for his line of work, and he wields an explosive temper and a mouth fit for a sailor. He resembles a violent
Italian Popeye from New Jersey. Paulie has worked his way
up in the business for thirty years. He's a veteran soldier.

Given the Christian name of Peter Paul Gualtieri, he bears
the name of the infamous Apostle Paul. Paul was a radical
Pharisee, a soldier of the Jewish law, and a killer of Christians.
After Paul's spiritual transformation, in which Christ spoke to
him audibly through a bright light that blinded him for three
days, he must have been deeply shamed and disgusted by his
career of hatred and violence. The Scriptures speak of Paul's
"thorn in the flesh," a pain that would not leave him. Many
have pondered the source of the pain that plagued the prolif-
ic author of the majority of the New Testament.

Like the Apostle, Paulie has issues of his own. When Tony
gathers the troops to confess he is seeing a psychiatrist,
Paulie admits to seeing a therapist as well. The brutal acts he
committed haunt him and draw him into therapy, then into
the bizarre living room of a psychic who claims to "channel"
the spirits of the men Paulie has slain. And he has slain many
a man. The psychic sees dozens of spirits spouting hateful
messages to their killer. The faces of the people he has killed
will not leave him. They appear in his thoughts and dreams
and torment his criminal routine. Is it possible that Paulie
Walnuts shares his sorrow and conviction?

Paulie believes in God, but sadly, he places his faith in outward compliance instead of inward transformation. During one episode, Paulie confronts his priest about his troubles. He is being tormented by the thought that there is a spiritual realm, and in that realm his victims have united in hatred against him. He blames the priest, saying, "I should have had immunity to all of this shit on the count of all my donations." He believes contributions to his church should cover a multitude of sins. His greedy priest seems to have missed the Vatican's memo passed down about 500 years ago on the subject of abolishing the sale of indulgences.

Paulie is much more like his other apostolic namesake, Peter. Although Peter bitterly defended his boss against Roman soldiers, even to the point of cutting off one soldier's ear, He denies him thrice when things go bad. Will Paulie repent and seek authentic spiritual transformation? If he does, he will have to deny Tony and the criminal life he has been leading.

Silvio

Silvio Dante serves as consigliere for the Soprano crime family and owner/operator of New Jersey's Bada Bing strip club, a frequent hangout of local mobsters. Silvio spends his days working the streets and following orders. He had dreams of working in show business, possibly becoming the next Sinatra. Instead he searches for a different kind of talent, young girls willing to dance naked in his clubs. He could have been an actor; after all, he does a great Pacino imitation, "Just when I thought I was out ... they pulled me back in." His wife, Gabriella, loves and supports him, but his daughter, Heather, is less than accepting of the exploitation of women at the strip club. Silvio defends it, saying, "These girls bring home $1500 a week." But this carries no weight with his little princess.

Silvio is well liked and well connected with a very diverse group of people. He introduces Tony to a Hassidic Jew, Sholomo, who owns a motel. Sholomo's son-in-law is abusing his wife and trying to shake down Sholomo for 50 percent of his motel income. Sholomo turns to Tony and agrees to give him 25 percent to use his persuasive power. During a not-so-friendly visit by Silvio, Paulie, and Tony, this Hassidic tough guy stands his ground and defends himself with a history lesson, "Two years, 900 Jews held their own against 15,000 Roman soldiers. They chose death before enslavement; and the Romans, where are they now?" Tony replies, "You're looking at them." With threats of emasculating Sholomo's son-in-law and their knee in his face, the Romans win the standoff.

Silvio appears to be friendly. With his slicked back tall fifties-style haircut, odd sense of humor, and passive demeanor he seems like a likable guy; but make no mistake, he is violent. When a stripper at the club borrows money for her braces then skips work he doesn't vacillate. Silvio plants his fist in her face.

Pussy

Salvatore Bonpensiero, better known as "Big Pussy," completes Tony's trinitarian inner circle of friends. This 350-pound soldier is a stone-cold gangster, but could easily be the most congenial character on this fictional mob hit. He's a loveable family man with three college-aged kids and a faithful wife. He was described by Detective Vin Makasian as a man who loved his family above all else. Pussy's been a friend of the family since Tony's childhood. He worked with Johnny Boy, Tony's dad, long before he served on Tony's crew. He and Tony go way back.

These men have history. They've shared life. Pussy's the last guy you'd think would be "flipped." As Pussy admits, though, "Sometimes you gotta do things you don't wanna do." Pussy gets overloaded. College tuition, high mortgage, escalating bills, it all becomes too much for him, an excruciating stretch. He starts moving heroine to bring in a little extra cash. Then Pussy strolls into the FBI's trap. Trafficking H brings a mandatory twenty-five years to life imprisonment, but he was offered a two-year sentence in exchange for information that would convict Tony Soprano.

Pussy turns government witness. This information comes like a cannon blast at the end of the first season. Tony's best friend has betrayed him. It takes another year before the whole truth comes out, but in the end it's a truth people the world over were forced to swallow. When Makasian delivers the sad news to Tony about Pussy's conversion to the other side, he apologizes saying, "I'm sorry, I know you like him." Tony replies, "Like him. I fucking love him!" These men weren't only buddies. They were brothers. Family.

This was more than just business. It was a family crisis. Pussy was Anthony Junior's godfather, and it's this man who sold his friend out for an easier life and a shorter sentence. He's the Judas Iscariot of the New Jersey mob. Judas Iscariot was one of the twelve men Jesus chose to share His life with. A soldier to Christ. A follower in faith. A part of the family. The Bible says he sold the Messiah out for thirty pieces of silver, just a little cash to make the road ahead a bit smoother.

Judas and Salvatore "Big Pussy" Bonpensiero shared the same fate. Both men died miserable and alone. Pussy was murdered by his three best friends, the ones he betrayed. Judas used his money to buy a field; it was there he ended his own life by hanging himself on tree. The Bible says in gruesome detail that "his body burst open and all his intestines spilled out."[2] This is not much different than Pussy's bloody execution. Tony, Silvio, and Paulie took him on a boat and sailed out to sea. They ushered him into the cabin, and ten seconds later each of them pulled out their guns and shot Pussy repeatedly in the chest. One shot after another until he was almost in pieces. A sad parting of old friends. Ironically, Salvatore means "the one who saves."

BETRAYED WITH A KISS

"Love, either towards God or man, is an affair of the will."
—C.S. Lewis

All men have choices to make about love.

Choosing to love someone is assuming a place of comforting weakness and beautiful vulnerability. When someone enters the realm of true emotion and deep affection, there is the potential for confidence to be violated and love returned with betrayal. As we open ourselves up to the joys of love, we are at the same time leaving ourselves open to rejection. The same is true in *The Sopranos*. Love and commitment bind the Soprano families; and in that bond, they often choose to be disloyal and break the vows of marriage, friendship, and criminal covenant.

Tony and seemingly the entire male population in New Jersey deceive their wives with girlfriends (goomars) and strippers, most with no moral remorse. With Tony it's always a struggle. He loves Carmela but is overtaken with lust for his twenty-four-year-old Russian mistress. In violating the vow he made to his wife on their wedding day, Tony is destroying his family. James, the brother of Christ, offers this equation for the destructive power of sin, "Each one is tempted when, by his own evil desire, he is dragged away and enticed. Then, after desire has conceived, it gives birth to sin; and sin, when it is full-grown, gives birth to death."[2] This is proven true with Tony. He is tempted to betray his wife by sleeping with another woman. This evil desire (to betray his wife) lures him into his girlfriend's bed and he is enticed. The evil desire gives birth to sin: infidelity. And his sin, when it is full-grown (when he hits rock bottom or when his wife has had enough) gives birth to the death of his marriage.

Betrayal and love are inseparably linked. John Le Carre, the twentieth century British author says in *The Perfect Spy*, "Betrayal can only happen if you love." Tony's love of his families has set him up for the pain of treachery. The tension that exists between the vow Tony made to his wife and his desire for his young girlfriend is ravaging his family and business. He continues to make promises that he is not capable of keeping. So he betrays his wife and children, his girlfriend, his clan, and himself. For these reasons Christ taught that it is unwise to take an oath. All of these promises have made Tony a betrayer as well. He claims the core values of their Italian-American gangster lifestyle are honor, loyalty, and family. These ideals are unrecognizable in the day-to-day life of New Jersey's depressed Mafioso.

What is honor among criminals? Respect among the unlawful? In the mafia, it is everything, a matter of life and death. A man without honor is a man unprotected, out in the open, a visible target. It is strange that men, whose life purpose is to break the laws established by the broader culture, will only survive by abiding by the laws of this thing they are a part of. Honor is inseparably linked to fear and self-preservation in this criminal underworld. It is not honor, for honor's sake. Al Capone said in one interview, "People who respect nothing dread fear. It is upon fear, therefore, that I have built up my organization. Those who work with me are afraid of nothing. Those who work for me are kept faithful, not so much because of their pay as because they know what might be done with them if they broke faith."[3]

Tony leads a group of seemingly fearless men. Undaunted, they attack a throng of African-American protesters with clubs and chains; the feds are breathing down their neck; enemies plot to kill them. They seem unafraid, but they are not truly fearless. As Capone says, the thing they ultimately fear is what would happen to them if they were disloyal to the family. Like Pussy Bonpensiero, one day he is drinking a Heineken with the boss and the next he's sleeping with the fishes.

Pussy was the last person Tony ever thought would hurt him, but it's Tony's best friend who is working hard to put him in jail, broadcasting their criminal interactions in full bandwidth to the FBI. When Pussy betrays his vow, it is more than Tony could endure. Tony's naturally explosive temper and violent threats quickly turn to sorrow and depression. A man he deeply loves is killed, the blood is fresh on Tony's hands, and there is no wake or safe place to mourn the loss. Pussy is sleeping with the fishes. The strong, commanding Mafioso shuts down, sleeps all day, and mourns another love lost. In despair, Tony turns to delusions, creating a woman in his mind named Isabella who is simple, loyal, and true. She's the mother he dreamed of but never had. Some men have erotic fantasies; Tony dreams only of a loving mother.

Tony fantasizes about a loving mother because he's never had one. Livia instigates an assassination attempt on her only son, while Tony's uncle waits for confirmation of Tony's death. Viewers are asking in disbelief, "How can this be real?" But it is. We live in a world where mothers murder their children, siblings shoot one another, and children commit mass murder. Tony survives the assault of the two young hit men, but the wound inflicted by evidence of his mother's betrayal on FBI tapes is absolutely incurable. He loves her, and she has rebuffed his affection with cruelty. In this show, a man can't even trust his own mother. Pussy, the betrayer, says it best, "Forget your enemies; you can't even depend on your friends."

Tony seeks revenge on his mother and attempts to suffocate her with a pillow. Ancient Scripture speaks truth into a new millennium, "With treachery the treacherous betray!"[4] It is only logical that men and women committed to crime, greed, and self-interest will hold to those values. These people spend their entire lives deceiving and hurting people, and in time they are destined to turn on one another. In broken and betrayed lives, people seek loyalty and commitment, but the devotion they find is only temporary if not found in the eternal love of God of Abraham, Isaac, and Jacob. There is only one who does not fail. Men will let you down; even great men stumble; but the Creator of heaven and earth loves unconditionally. This God declares, "I will be with you; I will never leave you nor forsake you."[5] And in the New Testament the stakes are raised, "If we are faithless, [God] will remain faithful."[6]

These pillars (honor, loyalty, and family) are crumbling quickly for *The Sopranos*, and the walls are coming down. The foundation is greed and it is flawed. There is a longing for days gone by, a simpler time when "yes" meant "yes" and "no" meant "no," but maybe there were no good old days. Jesus spoke of betrayal 2000 years ago saying, "You will be betrayed even by parents, brothers, relatives, and friends, and they will put some of you to death."[7] These words ring true for Tony and the families.

Loyalty to an organization and its boss is what makes organized crime work, but a loyalty rooted in fear will eventually collapse. Tony realizes his scare tactics are no longer working. One man after another embraces Tony, proclaiming deep devotion. Then devotion turns to jealousy and greed, and each one hastily looks for an opportunity to place a dagger in Tony's back. The seventeenth century French memoirist and philosopher Francis duc de la Rochefoucauld said, "It is more shameful to distrust one's friends than to be deceived by them." Welcome to the family.

ANGER: THE GUN THAT ALWAYS BACKFIRES

Like the Bible, *The Sopranos* says a lot about anger. The characters in the show fixate on jealousy, revenge, and righting injustice. But all anger is not the same. Richie Aprile assaults Beansy, a restaurant owner, in a murderous rage and runs him over repeatedly with his car. Beansy, a good earner and long-time friend to Tony, suffers a broken back. Tony defends his friend and demands that Richie build handicap ramps for Beansy's house. It's the least he can do. The resentment Tony has against Richie is justified. But Tony's anger can get out of hand as well. In defense of a dead young stripper, Tony looses his anger against a foolish soldier who killed the young mother in a drug-induced rage, and it is beautiful. When he grabs that man, lifting him up by the collar ready to strike, viewers embrace his righteous anger and rejoice. This is what it is like to arouse the anger of God.

God, the main character in the Bible, is the angriest person in the sacred narrative. The prophet Isaiah claims repeatedly that when God looks at evil, "His anger is not turned away."[8] This anger that burns within the God of Scripture is passionate and beautiful. But God's anger is easily misunderstood, and too often misconstrued. Apart from God's anger, His love means nothing. His wrath brings forth new life, and in His rage love is manifest. God's anger seeks out sin, injustice, and unrighteousness, and replaces the profane with the sacred.

David Powlison says, "The crimes that arouse God's wrath

are capital crimes: betrayal, rebellion, deceit, and blasphemous beliefs. The human heart is treacherous; we desire to believe *anything* but what is really true about God. The feelings aroused in us when we hear someone described by the word 'traitor' give a hint of the reasoning within God's wrath. Human beings were intended to listen to God's life-giving voice and to treat one another with love. But we have hearts of stone. We are headstrong."

Man's anger is not so noble. Everyone gets angry, but too often our ire is aroused by trivial transgression and small-minded beliefs. Then, for all the wrong reasons, people lash out with the intent to injure. Janice Soprano is declaring her undying love to her fiancée and soul mate, Richie Aprile. Then, without warning, anger gives birth to aggression within her. When a crude joke escalates, Richie punches Janice in the teeth. She reaches for a pistol and shoots him repeatedly. Is this justifiable anger at work?

Most often selfishness is the fuel for our anger. A jab at the ego, perceived offense, and inconvenience light the match of our fury, not genuine issues of injustice. For instance, most people raise their blood pressure in traffic, furious when someone cuts them off, but are barely able to feign interest in the epidemic of AIDS in Africa, abuse of families and children in Sudan, or even ethnic cleansing. So we smolder in the petty offenses of life and family and ignore real brutality across the world.

Fear and anger are first cousins, and they typically reside

together. For instance, Tony screams at A.J. for breaking a plate loaded with food, berating his son in front of his mother. Is he angry about the plate? No. He is fearful Anthony has already become like him, eating constantly to ignore his pain. Tony's anger revealed a deeper truth: he's afraid Anthony Junior will turn out like his old man.

Instead of loving God and neighbor, we allow our priority, above all else, to become loving ourselves. But this love of self deceives when we are feeding our own incessant appetites. On the surface it appears that our depression and rage are rooted in a low self-esteem (a lack of self love), when in reality the rage comes from our own arrogance and self-centeredness (the epitome of self love). Emptiness and isolation are the end result.

The ensuing insecurity is then described as self-loathing, but it is anything but. In actuality it is a self-obsession that always wonders what the rest of the world thinks about the clothes we wear, our prestige, and how we live. Tony lives in this abyss of self-obsession, trying to appease two families around him and come out as the good guy. It seldom works.

King David warns us, "In your anger, do not sin."[10] He knew when the adrenaline begins to rush, words begin to fly, and actions are taken in haste, people do foolish things. The disappointments of a fallen world clash with our hopes and dreams. It seems natural then to strike back in anger and irritation. The Bible speaks to this problem of anger that can so easily consume and destroy the whole person. Anger eats at your psyche like a cancer and destroys the body and immune system systematically. Popular teachings dismiss anger as an occurrence that builds up inside a person, an emotion that is separate from the whole being. This is not true; anger is not an emotion separate from the whole person. Instead, anger is an indicator, like warning lights in your automobile, of the existence of a problem within. It exposes the true condition of the heart. It is a part of who we are, and it reveals our self-ishness, impatience, and greed.

HEALING AN INFECTION OF THE SOUL

"Get rid of all bitterness, rage and anger, brawling and slander, along with every form of malice." —Ephesians 4:31

The remedy for the anger so prevalent in life and in *The Sopranos* is clear. However, an antidote so easily identified is often the most difficult thing to carry out. The pain and torment Tony lives in is not truly inflicted by his mother, but by his unwillingness to forgive his mother. Some would say she does not deserve to be forgiven. And they'd be right. This wicked and cruel woman seems incapable of love and joy; she does not even seek restitution. But forgiving his mother is what is best for Tony, not for Livia. Releasing his anger and resentment would clear his head and lighten his soul, which carries a heavy load.

Tony suffers for holding onto the wrongs committed against him, like the rest of humanity that also functions in a subdued ire. Resentment builds up like an infection in the soul, and in a moment of anxiety the toxic rage is spewed out on a loved one or unsuspecting stranger. Tony cannot understand his uncontrollable fury. Things are going well, his enemies have been squelched and wealth abounds. So why is he tearing phones out of walls and berating his son in a vulgar frenzy? It is because he clings to a lifetime of offense, refusing to release the pain and be granted a new start.

The anger feels good to Tony; it sparks a rush of adrenaline like a drug. He excuses his desire to live this life of anger, saying, "You gotta direct your anger where it belongs." He believes it can be used to his advantage; if anger could be used as a weapon against the people who deserve his fury, then it would be an asset and serve a useful purpose. But anger is like a gun that always backfires. What Tony is describing is revenge. For Tony, revenge seems like the only prescription to heal betrayal. He kills Pussy and drops him in the ocean, shoots the Bevalaqua kid for assaulting Christopher, and even attempts to smother his mother to bring restitution. Sin leads to more sin. And then more death.

True healing cannot be found in murderous revenge. That is why the Apostle Paul encourages us to "be kind and compassionate to one another, forgiving each other, just as in Christ God forgave you."[11] God has forgiven mankind unconditionally, time after time. In a human sense, this kind of forgiveness seems impossible. Turning the other cheek and moving beyond the offense means letting go of the pain and seeking a new joy in life. This can often be difficult, like forgiving Jesus Rossi, the young pervert who raped Dr. Melfi; or Don Hauser, the soccer coach/pedophile; or Ralphie, the sadistic and fiery capo. None of them deserve forgiveness. They have not earned it. But that is the point. Forgiveness is about breaking the cycle, and choosing a path of peace and health.

THE FUTILITY OF LIFE
FOR EVERYTHING THERE IS A SEASON

Mankind spends a lifetime chasing after things more difficult to catch than the wind. The wealth and riches he acquires become a source of worry and fear. Protecting the money, houses, and cars is taxing and he holds no guarantees that the heirs to this fortune will not spend it foolishly. They could squander it and the fruits of a lifetime of toil and labor would go up in smoke.

America is marked by its protestant work ethic and consumption-driven culture. These two go hand in hand. Men work long hours, and why? So they can buy more stuff: window coverings, big screen televisions, designer couches, and PlayStation2s. These things do not bring contentment. Yet they become our purpose, our gods. Life is about working so we can have more things, achieve a level of status, and get that nifty five percent cash rebate from Discover. This empty way of life is leading industrialized nations to the brink of internal collapse. Our consumption is destroying the environment; the economy must be propped up by credit cards and incentives that keep everyone spending. We're buying things on borrowed money that will come due after the thrill of the expenditure has long worn off. Yet we still buy and remain unhappy. People are questioning this endless circle and looking for an escape route. Wealth is empty, and the things that are real and life giving (spirituality, family, nature, and beauty) are neglected and often noticeably absent. The wisest man who ever lived articulated the struggle this way:

> "There is a time for everything,
> And a season for every activity under heaven:
> You're born and you die,
> You plant and you uproot,
> You kill and you heal,
> Tear down and build back up again,
> You weep and then laugh,
> Mourn and dance,
> Scatter stones only to gather them again,
> You embrace then refrain from embracing,
> There is a time to search and a time to give up,
> A time to keep and a time to throw away,
> A time to tear and a time to mend,
> A time to be silent and a time to speak,
> A time to love and a time to hate,
> A time for war and a time for peace
> What do we gain from this endless circle?"

This song, written by King Solomon (later turned pop hit by The Birds), paints the picture of the meaningless nature of our existence. Solomon prefaced the song by saying, "I hated all the things I had toiled for under the sun, because I must leave them to the one who comes after me. And who knows whether he will be a wise man or a fool? Yet he will have control over all the work into which I have poured my effort and skill under the sun. This too is meaningless."[2] Tony is familiar with these thoughts. He works to attain wealth and power that may be squandered and lost in an instant. His death is always imminent. Indictments that could ensure that his days would end behind bars are probable and the teenage boy he will leave in his stead has to be picked up from summer camp for wetting the bed. These fears lead to depression and anxiety. Solomon called this despair of heart, which leads to a hatred of life.

Futility cannot be disputed; gathering and storing up wealth is meaningless. The best thing a man can do, according to Solomon, is to eat his food, drink his wine, and be merry. Enjoy the life given to you. Give honor to the Creator who gives you these blessings. Raise your glass to family, friends, and loved ones. Enjoy them because life is brief and joy is fleeting.

The Hebrews subscribed to a school of thought that believed in a dualist universe. They believed and taught that everything above the sun was divine, invisible, other, separate, the home of God and that everything under the sun was natural, visible, touchable, apart from God, the home of man. Everything under the sun is meaningless. Apart from an infinite Creator, nothing has purpose. If dying was it, what's the point? Why work? Why gather riches? Why start a family? Why love? There has to be more.

THE SEARCH FOR DIVERSIONS

"If our condition were truly happy we should not need to divert ourselves from thinking about it." —Blaise Pascal

While observing the futility of man's days, Solomon commented, "All his days his work is pain and grief; even at night his mind does not rest. This too is meaningless." Tony can sympathize. Tony lives under the burden of the futility of his life and work, always questioning his purpose, and never understanding the meaning of his existence. He works illegally in a dangerous career to buy things he doesn't need (i.e. $20,000 fur coat, $80,000 Mercedes, et cetera) only to leave them to a lazy son and an ungrateful daughter. But Tony keeps working and keeps acquiring because it's a diversion to keep him from acknowledging this endless circle of meaningless life under the sun. But the diversions don't satisfy; they leave him feeling emptier than ever.

Peter Kreeft reminds us, "Freud, in *Civilization and Its Discontents*, asks why we are not happier than our ancestors, since our technology has made us like gods and fulfilled nearly every fairy-tale wish and wishful thinking that invented the gods in the first place. He simply can't find out why we wielders of godlike knowledge and power are not happier than our ignorant and impotent ancestors." Freud's question is not unlike our own.

We live in a world and time of over-priced, complex diversions. We have at our fingertips a million different distractions to make us forget about a million different things. Ours is a life of overstocked medicine cabinets, high-speed Internet connections, bombarding corporate advertising campaigns, satellite television, and mind-numbing techno music. Silence is golden, and it has escaped the western world. The grinding noise that fills our ears and the chaos that over stimulates us has overtaken once sacred space.

Because of our sin and the bondage we've been in since the fall of man, the reality of our lives is overwhelming and painful, and that pain is exacerbated by our selfish choices. The most "holy" individuals still live in the thralls of their own private prison of secret sins. C.S. Lewis expressed this sentiment, saying, "We are not necessarily doubting that God will do the best for us; we are wondering how painful the best will turn out to be."[6] The book of Job teaches us that even the best people who love their family, neighbor, and God are not exempt from pain and suffering. But there is still hope.

Often the pain itself is trying to teach us something, like an ache deep in our body crying out for relief. There is a disease here that requires treatment. The difficulties each person faces in life offer opportunities to learn how to live better, make more intelligent choices, and recognize moral truths. It is only by pushing through the pain that answers are found. Facing the conflict, turmoil, and relational brokenness in our lives is a discipline that must be learned.

If happiness were prevalent there would be no need to live life in the midst of revolving diversions, but we seek to avoid the sting of life by becoming absorbed with pleasure, empty tasks, and anything that numbs real feeling. The obvious come to mind. Drugs. Violence. Sex. Art, music, and film often fill the space of our lives simply to distract us from the tasks that lie before us. Why dwell on the fact we are unable to pay our American Express bill, and that our college loans are set on a forty-year schedule? It is easier to just go to the movies. Some diversions are healthy, a natural break from the monotony of life. When one leaves the theater refreshed and ready to address his financial problems, the time away has served him well. But some leave the theater in search of the next diversion. Then life becomes a series of endless distractions.

Tony's office, the infamous Bada Bing, is a strip club. Daily business is done as girls dance naked around poles while miserable men stuff five-dollar bills in the panties of these young girls and drink four-dollar shots. The entire room lit with pink and blue lights. This is ultimate diversion. To reward themselves on a good day, the men get a blowjob. But this is not reality; it's an illusion, a myth built to forget about an angry boss, a nagging wife, disobedient kids, and a low-paying job. They choose to pay for diversions rather than face the truth and seek the redemption found in confronting their problems. But redemption is out there, waiting to be found. As Christ said, "Seek, and you shall find."

Pascal said, "The only thing that consoles us for our miseries is diversion. And yet it is the greatest of our miseries. For it is above all which prevents us thinking about ourselves and leads us imperceptibly to destruction. But for that we should be bored, and boredom would drive us to seek some more solid means of escape, but diversion passes our time and brings us imperceptibly to our death."

Boredom is inescapable, but the oddest activities are enough to mask it: everything from lap dances at the Bada Bing to a warm plate of baked ziti covered with mozzarella. Diversions come in many forms. When these activities no longer work, one turns to sex, wine, cocaine, exercise of power, and Prozac to numb the pain. At some point it all fails to be an adequate diversion for Tony. He describes the strange discontent of watching an otherwise good movie, *Seven*. But he knows this makes no real difference in his life and admits to Dr. Melfi, "This is bullshit, a waste of my fucking time. Why do I give a shit who the killer is?" All the tasks that occupy his time are meaningless. They are only a series of distractions until death. All of the commotion only delays the inevitable. At some point he must contemplate the state of his life and face the challenges that await him. A.J. also exemplifies the basic human tendency to seek diversion; he deadens the blow of reality by sinking himself into video games, pornography, and the Internet, connecting to a life other than his own.

We search for happiness and make it our goal. Tony even equates his work in therapy with the potential he has to be happier. This longing for utter bliss goes unfulfilled, but instead of contemplating the source of despair and a possible remedy, man runs to anything that will occupy his mind and drown his depression. A cure for wretchedness, death, and

selfishness cannot be found apart from God, so we must journey toward the eternal and walk toward the divine. This pilgrimage requires stillness when motion is irresistible and
silence when noise is pleasing. In this contemplative space,
void of distractions, God speaks. And if man is still and quiet
enough, he will hear.

*"Throw moderation to the winds, and the greatest pleasures bring
the greatest pains."* —Democritus

HEDONISM, HOOKERS, AND HALF-TRUTHS

A five-course meal with a glass of red wine, Cuban cigars, and
thirty-year-old scotch are all just a part of the daily routine
for Tony Soprano, the narcissistic King Pin who chooses to
spend his waking hours immersed in continuous self-pleas-
ure. He drinks Cognac, smokes a cigar, and gets a professional blowjob from a young stripper all at the same time.
Like King Solomon, Tony denies himself nothing. If he
wants it, he has it. And Tony has it all: the house, the cars, the
pool, a sixty-foot yacht, and more pleasure than the average
man can imagine. Yet still he searches for more.

Tony is a hedonist. He may not know what the word means,
but he is one. The ancient Greek philosopher Epicurus (341-
270 B.C.) developed the idea of ethical hedonism. This philosophy of life is about avoiding pain and embracing pleasure. It's very simple: Pain is bad and pleasure is good.

In a letter to Menoeceus, Epicurus wrote, "We recognize

pleasure as the first good innate in us, and from pleasure we begin every act of choice and avoidance, and to pleasure we return again, using the feeling as the standard by which we judge every good."[10] Epicurus believed if you reduced the number of your desires they could be more easily managed. For instance, instead of lusting after candy, sex, espressos, cheesecake, and fine cigars, one should focus their desires only on sex and fine cigars. Epicurus believed this might be a more attainable goal. Tony, like the consumerist culture he lives in, has not mastered this fine art. Tony wants it all, and he gets it all; but it yields him no peace.

The mystique of pleasure wanes quickly and leaves a person confused and self-consumed. The orgasm is too short lived and the caffeine buzz that comes from expensive chocolate never satisfies our insatiable appetite. It only postpones the sting of reality. Pain is inevitable; avoiding it is only delaying a complete breakdown until another day. When a lifetime of problems comes calling, it comes on heavy and with devastating power. Solomon found this to be true and wrote, "I thought in my heart, 'Come now, I will test you with pleasure to find out what is good.' But that also proved to be meaningless' And what does pleasure accomplish?'"

Hedonists are only getting half the truth. Pleasure is a gift from a loving God. When the Creator is taken out of the picture and pleasure becomes the goal, it is empty, lonely, and meaningless. C.S. Lewis said, "The worst lie is the half-truth." J.I. Packer agrees, "A half-truth masquerading as the whole truth becomes a complete untruth." Satan sought to convince Adam and Eve of this half-truth and planted seeds of mistrust, leaving them to ponder what they must be missing. God directed them to refrain from eating the fruit of only one tree. Was God holding out on them and keeping the best for his own pleasure? Could God be trusted? Oswald Chambers said, "All sin is rooted in the suspicion that God is not very good." Some skeptics of faith believe God is some kind of holy dictator who despises the pleasure of man. There could be nothing further from the truth. His plan is for paradise, and it has been since the beginning.

In Eden, with all of its pleasures, Adam and Eve wanted more, and broke the rules trying to get it. In doing so, paradise was lost and mankind was expelled from the naked bliss of the all-you-can-eat fruit garden. The world has never been the same. Sin gave birth to death and a lifetime filled with pain. Tony, like the rest of the world, is trying to compel himself back to the garden by immersing himself in pleasure. Aged wine, fine cuisine, and adventurous sex remind us of what we have lost and transport the mind temporarily back to paradise. Sorrowfully, we end up tumbling back to a desolate reality with only the memory of a momentary ecstasy.

All that was pure and shameless in the garden has been distorted by humanity. Even a pleasure as beautiful as sex has become an unhealthy obsession. Patrick Carnes, a counselor in Michigan explains why: "Sexual fantasy is what many people use to cope with the inescapable loneliness of a tragic world racked with sin."[12] Sex: the great diversion. It is an attempt to force our way back to Eden to recover what has been lost. The elation of physical pleasure is like a taste of the divine. An act of beauty intended to draw two people to a place of total union, physical and spiritual oneness is instead used for cheap thrills. This pleasure hunt is driven by a need to escape the pain of a broken life. But God honors our choice. A modern proverb says, "Sin is man's way of telling God to leave him alone. Hell is God's way of saying okay." Harry Schaumburg describes it this way, "God's action is severe in that He gives us over not only to our desires but to a condition of ungovernable desires. We demand, God steps back. We choose to regulate our lives rather than honoring and obeying God; we lose the ability to regulate our desires."[13] If we pursue pleasure apart from God and His design, we are asking God to step back. Because He gave us free will to pursue our own desires, He honors our choice.

The Apostle Paul said, "Although they claimed to be wise, they became fools and exchanged the glory of the immortal God for images made to look like mortal man and birds and animals and reptiles. Therefore God gave them over in the sinful desires of their hearts."[14] Sooner or later we are owned by our desires and the illusion of control is gone. Pleasure is fleeting; only God remains.

SEXUALITY
LIKE A FULL GOBLET OF WINE

In the Soprano family it seems easy to imagine open and frank discussion about sexuality. If your dad's office is at a strip club, one would think that talk about the birds and the bees would be appropriate dinner table conversation. Not true at the Soprano table. When Meadow endorses legalized prostitution during a family discussion, Tony will have nothing do with it. Though he has plenty to do with prostitutes, the discussion is more than he can handle. Tony sets the ground rules that they will not talk about sex in his house, saying, "It may be the nineties out there, but in here it's 1954." The duality is unmistakable, and like in many families a choice is made to live in silence about the distinct and beautiful gift of sex. It seems the Don of New Jersey and the Church suffer from the same hypocrisy, by making a choice to keep quiet about the most obvious fact of creation. Mankind has been created with the potential to know utter joy and also possess the whole power of creation, pro-creation.

God is not bashful. He did not mask or disguise His sexual

creation. In fact, anatomically, the distinctions are quite clear. The Bible is not afraid of sex either. It is clear in the Song of King Solomon that within God's plan, sex is to be celebrated. A shameless God has entrusted the Scriptures to a bashful people who would like to return with Tony Soprano to 1954, the good old days when Ward and June Cleaver slept in separate beds.

Even translators of the Bible hide from the beautiful literature describing sexual love. In the seventh chapter of Solomon's Song, the cowardice of the English translators is evident. Solomon sings of the splendor of his wife's body, beginning with her feet, "Your sandaled feet are beautiful, and your legs are perfectly defined, as if sculpted..." And he is just warming up. Working his way up her body, he exclaims, "Your vagina is always wet, like a full goblet of wine." This was quite a compliment in the days before KY Jelly, and its presence in the cannon of Scripture affirms God's gift of sexual union as beautiful. But either in fear of public opinion or out of sheer embarrassment, the translators of Scripture refer to her genitals as her navel. Have you ever known a woman with a wet navel? The power of sex is so daunting these translators intentionally mislead their readers.

It would be better to return to the garden, a place where sexuality was not shameful. God looked on Adam and Eve as the two became one, and Scripture says, "The man and his wife were both naked, and they felt no shame."[1] In the new millennium sex is no longer taboo. And this is good. However, instead of choosing sex in the context of love, commitment, and beauty—sex that is shameless—culture has chosen immediate gratification. This world of orgasms on demand is played out in Internet imagery, one-night stands, and sex in exchange for money. The Bada Bing, the girlfriends, and the casual sexual encounters paint a horrid picture of this divine gift. This is not the intention of the Creator of heaven and earth. His picture is much more beautiful.

Sex, in the context of marriage, makes available a security found no other place. In *The Sopranos*, this matrimonial refuge is laced with the hypocrisy of the Italian macho sexuality. This is explored in an episode called "Boca," where Junior is humiliated when the news spreads he has performed oral sex on a woman. Tony mocks his love-struck uncle as the old man who "is whistling through the wheat field." These men believe if a man will "suck pussy, he will suck anything." This is half homophobia and half machismo selfishness. A group of men who show up at the office (Bada Bing) and drop their drawers and a Ben Franklin for every stripper who comes in the place are somehow morally opposed to pleasuring their own spouses. They must have all missed Sunday school when the teacher taught it was greater to give than to receive. Although cunnilingus is rarely cited in Sunday school teachers' curriculums, you can find it in the Bible. Solomon's lover begs of him, "Blow on my garden that its fragrance may spread abroad. Let my lover come into his garden, and taste its choice fruits."[2] However, Tony and his crew are much less poetic than Solomon's lover when discussing this topic. In the marriage bed, pleasure is not simply self-serving; it is the fruit of an unswerving relationship to each other and to God. Like the commitment between God and His people, so is the commitment between a husband and his wife. For richer, for poorer, in sickness and in health, to love and to cherish as long as you both shall live. In this promise two people, under God, find a refuge in one another. It's more than ten minutes of elation; it is a lifetime of promise.

THE GOOSE AND THE GANDER

Men

A male fan of *The Sopranos* might easily admit he wants to be just like Tony Soprano, and his friends to be like Tony's crew. Maybe not quite as violent or abusive or unlawful, but a man who is tough and secure, a strong leader, a man people listen to, who has a team to back him up. Tony and the boys ignite a deep desire within all men to be aggressive, to take what they want. It would be exhilarating for them to actually say what they think, go at their enemies, and have people fear them and their power. However, compared to Tony, most men live lives of utter passivity. Our day may start out just like his, by walking outside in our bathrobe to get the paper, but usually the similarities end there.

Tony embodies the most exciting parts of manhood. He lives dangerously as a vigilante, taking the law into his own hands. When Coach Aubrey, Meadow's soccer coach, sleeps with one of the eleventh grade girls on his soccer team, Tony can take care of it. When Melfi was raped in a parking garage, every person on this side of the screen was aching for Tony to find out what had happened and render justice. There is joy that comes from this kind of power, a rest that comes from knowing wrongs can be made right and that revenge is only a phone call away.

Sadly, American men have bought into the retail marketing philosophy of stores like The Gap that says life is not gender specific, what is good for the goose is good for the gander. But the feminization of American men is wreaking havoc in the soul of the male species, who long for something more, something wild, a life beyond colorful rooms filled with stylish furniture from the Pottery Barn and cozy pictures hanging on every wall. Men desire adventure. Society is calling men to be more domesticated, yet most men would rather be like Rocky Balboa than George Costanza. Women don't want weak, passive men; it's the strong men who are irresistible, men who know when to defend and when to comfort. Tony beckons this deep desire of masculinity within all viewers, men who desire to be strong, and women looking for an anchor that is not so easily blown and tossed by the wind. Christian counselor John Eldredge says it well, "[Men always hear,] 'Be Nice. Be Swell. Be like Mother Theresa.' I'd much rather be told to be like William Wallace [from the movie Braveheart]."[3] Men are hungry to be men, not just women with penises.

There is tension in being a good man. It is the balance of possessing a gentle strength, being able to offer a strong hand of grace, being a warrior poet, leading with gentleness and being abusive or to threatening. King David knew we were made in the image and likeness of God, and that our masculinity should be mirrored to us from deity. David wrote: "One thing God has spoken, two things have I heard: that you, O God, are strong, and that you, O Lord, are loving."[4]

However, the view of masculinity in *The Sopranos* is vastly skewed. These gangsters are obsessed with power and strength and leave little room for grace or gentleness. Jesus said, "Blessed are the meek, for they will inherit the earth."[5] In the world of Tony Soprano, nothing is inherited; it is taken by force. Jesus continued: "Blessed are the merciful, for they will be shown mercy."[6] But here justice is valued over mercy. Extending grace is a sign a weakness. Tony mocks Carmela and the school for being overly concerned with Anthony Junior's feelings; he sees them as offering too much mercy. So he compensates with a strong hand of justice. Scriptures describes the kind of balance we should seek in the book of Micah: "To act justly and to love mercy." Men have become obsessed with justice, driven to blame someone for their hardships and to exact revenge. Nations become consumed with a tit-for-tat melee that allows no one to come out victorious. Tony, like many men (and leaders of nations), lacks a love for mercy, a joy in offering a gift of grace to someone else.

Real masculinity means taking initiative, making things happen, always admitting when you are wrong, and keeping a balance of strength and weakness. Culture has come to fear strong men when it is the weak men we should fear. Ritchie is a weak man, a loose cannon. He acts before he thinks, striking a two-bit gambler in front of high rollers and crippling the owner of a pizza parlor with his SUV—mindless acts that hurt the business and his own cause. Violence is not masculine. Tony, when he defends his son against an improper diagnosis or when he pins Ralphie to a wall seeking justice for the young stripper he murdered, displays the true positives of male strength. But Tony is often controlled by his temper, exploding in violent rage because his sandwich is missing from the refrigerator. Weak men prey on the helpless while living in a moral never-never land. This world is in desperate need of strong men. Men to lead families. Men to fight the real enemies. Men to restore a passion that has been lost far too long.

Women

"Boys are different from girls." —Big Pussy Bonpensiero

The Sopranos is widely loved despite its implausible treatment of the female gender. There is nothing redemptive or good about the view of women espoused in this show, nothing that praises women or acknowledges them as truly valuable and intelligent. Instead, these gangsters have made a covenant together as "made men" that their wives and families will never come first. And they keep that covenant by having sex with every woman possible, abandoning parental responsibilities, and risking the destruction of their own families through their infidelity and lies.

Words like "bitch" and "cunt" have become acceptable terms used to describe women on *The Sopranos*. This attitude and behavior is incessantly dreadful. But the most heinous aspect of this small-minded worldview is the violence that is commonly directed against women. In the third season, Ralphie beats a young stripper to death outside the Bada Bing. It would be intolerable art were it not for the fact that this is reality. There are men across the world who view women as disposable objects of pleasure to use or abuse. C.S. Lewis wrote, as if watching HBO on a Sunday evening, "A society in which conjugal infidelity is tolerated must always be in the long run a society adverse to women."[7] It is not only adverse to married women, but to all kinds of women.

These New Jersey Italian mobsters have allowed themselves to objectify women, minimizing the role of women into controlling categories.

The Madonnas

Tony's sister, Janice, tells Carmela, "They expect their wives to live like the fucking nuns at Mt. Carmel College." The faithful wives of the barbaric criminals represent loyalty, fidelity, purity, and family. These women stand by their husbands when leaving them would be fully justified. They're the Carmela Sopranos, the Angie Bonpensieros, the Gabriella Dantes, and the Rosalie Aprilis; the mothers of their children, the supporting pillars of the Cosa Nostra, the matriarchs of the family business. Janice points the finger to her sister-in-law, Carmela, as one who sells herself for the house, cars, and appliances. Why else would they stay with

these overweight men in jogging suits and black dress socks?
It is either the money or true love.

The Goomars

These women are the girlfriends, the sex toys, the some-
times-no-name vixens whom the men notice only for their
sexual gratification and minimal commitments. They are the
men's pastime. And there is usually no real dedication from
the men, no real commitment. The relationships are sus-
tained merely by the exchange of quickies and cash. But
these women are much more than prostitutes; the goomar is
a status symbol, and a relationship where these gangsters live
without the family man veneer.

The Messiahs

Not all women's value is found in their bodies or in their
ability to procreate. There are other females who aren't
thought of as whores or mothers, but rather as independent
woman who lead with strength and grace, women who possess great wisdom and intellect, women who speak softly and
comfort with a gentle hand yet dictate boldly and are able to
stand up to the boss. Women like Dr. Melfi and the dom of
the Italian mafia, Annalisa, Dr. Melfi's Italian counterpart.

The Devils

These women are scheming and detestable. Preying on
unsuspecting men, they are unpleasant, belligerent, back-
stabbing nags whom no one loves. Of Livia Soprano, one of
these women who is the source of Tony's pain, he says,
"You're dead to me." No one would want one of these

women as a goomar or a mother, and they offer no real wisdom or insight. Like Tony's sister Janice, they can never be trusted; their motives are always in question. Gloria, the psychotic Mercedes saleswoman, embodies this wickedness as she threatens, manipulates, and destroys everyone that comes into contact with her. They are evil to the core. Devils.

It is appalling how women are treated in this show. Richie Aprile holds a gun to Janice Soprano's head during sex. Janice confesses this violent fantasy to Carmela, who is aghast, and says, "I thought you were a feminist." Janice responds in her defense, "He usually takes the clip out." David Chase recalls convincing David Proval, who plays Richie, to do the shot despite the fact his wife was angry and disgusted with the scene and what it said about women. David Chase said, "We have not done a politically correct show yet, and we are not about to start now."[8] In this scene and others it seems commonplace to threaten physically and violently curse at a woman. Christopher pimp-slaps Adriana at a bar in front a room full of people when she mentions his drug use and no one even flinches. Her uncle Richie confronts Christopher and says, "I'm from the old school. You wanna raise your hand to her, give her your last name." Apparently in this business, hitting a woman becomes acceptable if you make vows you don't intend to keep.

Sadly, one quarter of American women are victims the worst kinds of violence, incest, and rape. Cowardly men prey on young girls in homes everywhere, everyday. American culture and the judicial system continue to fail these women. Pot smokers sit in jail while the majority of men who abuse their wives go unpunished. Prostitutes and strippers are killed on a daily basis with little concern or investigation. Some may argue that the show's vivid portrayal of violence against women glorifies this behavior, but that couldn't be further from the truth. On *The Sopranos*, brutality against women is seen for what it really is: the cowardice of weak men. Fearful men like Ralphie and Ritchie feel powerless in their unlawful vocation and seek to exercise domestic authority over women they claim to love. Intelligent viewers see this for what it is, needless violence feeding the egos of despicable men.

Tony almost seems like a hero for opposing Ralphie, who brutally kills the woman carrying his child. Ralphie sadistically acted out the common assumption that women at the Bada Bing are to bring pleasure and do not need to be treated as having real human value. The brutality is only a symptom rooted in the greater problem which relates to the value men place on a woman's intellect and well-being.

God created mankind, and as Adam saw the first woman totally naked before him, he sang to her, "You are flesh, of my flesh, for you are a part of me." The first woman was beautiful, and by her creation God gave man an opportunity to express love and affection. The men on *The Sopranos* should take heed. The women God created as their equals are not merely goomars, madonnas, whores, and devils. Let us not blame David Chase; he gets his inspiration from the real world. This is a culture in desperate need of change.

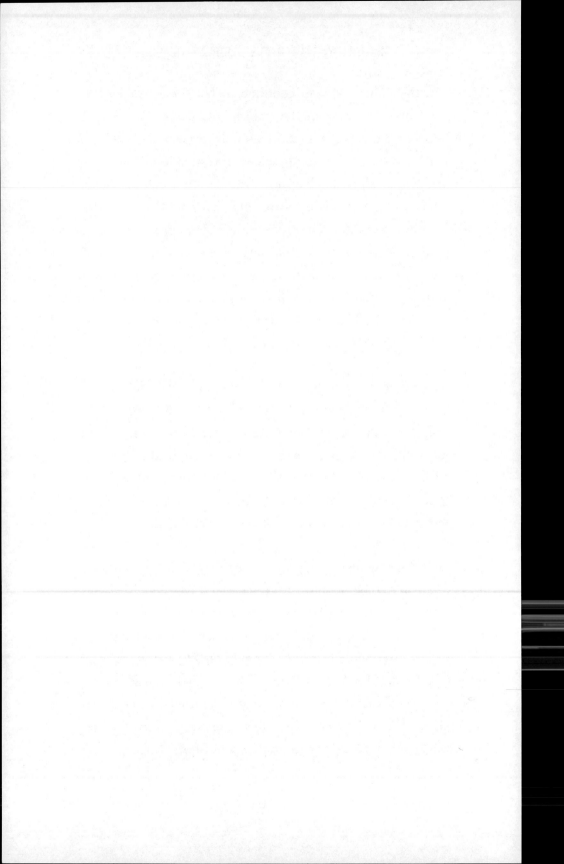

QUE SERA SERA
WHAT WILL BE, WILL BE

"Never say you hate life, that's blasphemy." —Christopher Moltisanti

Our world began with God breathing creation ex nihilo. He spoke and worlds were born; He breathed light and life into nothingness and formed man from the dust. God's hands have been working in mankind's midst since the beginning, and His plans cannot be frustrated by our own. The sacred words of Scripture declare, "For by him all things were created: things in heaven and on earth, visible and invisible, whether thrones or powers or rulers or authorities; all things were created by him and for him. He is before all things, and in him all things hold together."[1]

Tony tells his kids, "Only God can make a life." And he's right. It is God who creates, God who determines the outcome of events, and God who molds history and ordains the future. He is not bound by time or space. He is God over all, Creator of heaven and earth. You could not stop Him if you tried. Therefore, all must accept their place in the universe:

"Que sera sera," what will be will be.

For an assemblage of multiple-murderers and extortionists, this family has a remarkable confidence in the will of God. In a string of tribulations where Jackie Senior (and later Jackie Junior) dies, Artie Bucco loses his restaurant and almost his wife, Junior gets cancer, and Christopher faces death, no one blames or questions God. It is spoken and understood: "Que sera sera." God has allowed them to make choices that brought them to this place. Call it destiny. Call it fate. Call it divine will. It doesn't matter what you call it, that's just the way it is.

Christ instructed His followers to live a life of faith cognizant of God's control. In the burning heat of the Judean sun, Jesus stood on a hill and preached, "Who of you by worrying can add a single hour to his life?"[2] *The Sopranos* attempt to observe this ancient wisdom of Christ. In spite of their despicable acts and underworld schemes, Tony and the families seem to live in the tension between their longing for control and a belief in the sovereignty of God, exercising wisdom and grace and putting their hope in the One who authored faith and eternity. At times they are content with life, knowing that God is in control. And at others, without warning, they attempt to take the reigns of their own lives (as we all do).

In the swirling confusion of "I want it my own way" and "Thy will be done," these criminals cannot deny there is order amidst the chaos and redemption amidst their depravity. Though some like Christopher live in the delusion they could survive in the chaos alone, God quickly shatters the myth. Christopher avoids church and spirituality almost completely, but God reaches out to grab his attention, previewing his eternity in hell. Christ brings stability, offering Himself as the rock upon which to build and the anchor with which to gain security in the violent storms of life. The psalmist sang, "Our God is in heaven; he does whatever pleases him."[3] Yet some outcomes can be easily predicted, like the early death of the foolish wannabe gangster, Jackie Aprile. Dinner is interrupted at the Soprano house with the news of Jackie's death outside of the housing projects in Boonton. Tony turns to his young son, knowing Jackie's death could be a forewarning to A.J., and with a penetrating stare, says, "You see."

At times this criminal family accepts the truth that God is in control. They face life and death with an exact understanding of how God deals with His creation. They know finite will is no match for the infinite and perfect determination of the Maker of heaven and earth. Job knew this well and declared to God, "I know that you can do all things; no plan of yours can be thwarted."[4] What God chooses to do or not do cannot be undone or done. Death comes at a time of its own choosing. "Que sera sera." Tony's life is in God's hands. Carmela's health is in God's hands. Artie's marriage. Junior's illness. Christopher's fate. A.J.'s future. Life and death move with the resolve of a sovereign Creator who says, "What I have said, that will I bring about; what I have planned, that will I do."[5]

CONCLUSION

Some people watch this show with only half of their brain. One might walk away from an episode of *The Sopranos* and embrace the belief that money and pleasure bring happiness and contentment. They ignore the extreme guilt, paranoia, and greed that tears at each character, gradually ripping apart their lives. Many viewers have made this grand mistake.

Another person, however, might see through different eyes, denouncing the show as trash filled with sexual perversion and violence, while missing the greater art and beauty found in the tension between good and evil. The person doesn't see the wonderful mystery of God engaging men in their depravity. This is also a colossal mistake. This show is not mindless fodder. It is not a so-called reality peepshow, nor is it a Seinfeld-esque sitcom that creates comedy out of the trivialities of life. *The Sopranos* is a story so real, and explores matters so vital, that it incites a thoughtful response and it should not be taken lightly.

In a *Sopranos* message board on AOL, a young mother boasted of her love of the show. She claims her two-year-old daughter is now obsessed with *The Sopranos* and in fits of rage is only consoled by watching the show. Another woman logs in to agree; her young children think of Tony as a father. This is unbelievable. It is difficult to fathom what this does to young, impressionable minds and scary to think the next generation of children is being raised on Ritalin, day care, and *The Sopranos*. Vincent Pastore, who portrays Big Pussy

Bonpensiero says on a chat session transcript from HBO.com, "Kids shouldn't watch *The Sopranos*. I see children in my neighborhood and I'm shocked that their parents let them watch because of the sex, violence, and language."

This is adult content intended for those who have a solidified worldview. Without a strong sense of right and wrong, this story could destroy you. If the behavior of these families becomes normative, the show will have been an affront to a culture. Instead, if viewed with an open mind, *The Sopranos* has the potential to teach as parable about family, love, crime, and God.

The Hebrew people learned of the things of God and His Scripture through an exercise called "midrash." In a midrash it was believed real learning took place when tension was exposed, contrasting opposing views. Good parables create healthy tension. They subvert the viewer and bring troubling confusion that forces us to reexamine life, God, eternity, and what we believe. Like the parables of Jesus Christ, which were controversial and often confused the listeners and sparked debate and conversation, *The Sopranos* is the stuff of good midrash. F. Scott Fitzgerald describes it this way, "The test of a first-rate intelligence is the ability to hold two opposed ideas in the mind at the same time, and still retain the ability to function. One should, for example, be able to see that things are hopeless and yet be determined to make them otherwise." *The Sopranos* and David Chase spin that tension well. Chase does not offer the answers to life's questions; he only asks them in a way that forces all of us to grapple with them. It disturbs in a productive way. In the midst of this strain to examine life in light of this New Jersey parable, one might encounter God.

Tony, Carmela, Meadow, Christopher, Silvio, and Pussy are not heroes. Although many people will be tempted to glorify the lifestyle their characters represent, they should instead see them as they are, broken people, people looking for answers, people waking up each day and performing tasks while they search for meaning in it all. As you look past the cash and power and glamour they seem to posses, my hope is you will see yourself, as you are, acknowledge your longing to believe in something greater than yourself, and search for true answers. Answers to problems greater than your economic state, career problems, or relational brokenness. These answers bring healing, wholeness, and peace. Jesus says, "Seek and you will find."[1]

NOTES

INTRODUCTION
1 Mark 4:9

CHAPTER 1
2 Stephen Holden, *The New York Times on The Sopranos* (New York: iBooks, 2000), pg. XI.

2 Stephen Holden, *The New York Times on The Sopranos* (New York: iBooks, 2000), pg. XI.

3 Blaise Pascal, from Peter Kreeft's *Christianity for Modern Pagans* (Ft. Collins: Ignatius Press, 1993), pg. 58.

4 Ann Zivotsky, *North County Times* (March 22, 2001).

5 Hannah Brown, *The Jerusalem Post* (December 21, 2001).

6 Stephen Holden, *The New York Times on The Sopranos* (New York: iBooks, 2000), pg. XVIII.

7 Caryn James, *The New York Times on The Sopranos* (New York: iBooks, 2000), pg. 117.

8 Peter Kreeft, *Christianity for Modern Pagans* (Ft. Collins: Ignatius Press, 1993) pg. 51.

9 David Chase in an article by Robert Lloyd, "Mob Rules: David Chase on *The Sopranos*, the small screen, and rock & roll," *LA Weekly* (March 16 - 22, 2001).

10 David Chase in an article by Chris Heath, "Shocking Family Secrets: *Sopranos* Stars Tell All," *Rolling Stone* (March 29, 2001).

11 David Chase in an article by Robert Lloyd, "Mob Rules: David Chase on *The Sopranos*, the small screen, and rock & roll," *LA Weekly* (March 16 - 22, 2001).

12 *The New York Times*, "Critic's Choice, A Times Talks Series" video (TimesTalks Online).

13 *The New York Times*, "Critic's Choice, A Times Talks Series" video.

14 Jude Wanniski, who copied her memo to Lynn Cheney, posted on WorldNetDaily.com (http://www.worldnetdaily.com/news/archives.asp?AUTHOR_ID= 17&PAGE=4).

15 *The New York Times*, "Critic's Choice, A Times Talks Series" video.

CHAPTER 2

3 Stephen Holden, *The New York Times on The Sopranos* (New York: iBooks, 2000), pg. XV.

2 excerpted from *Saint of the Day*, revised edition (St. Anthony Messenger Press, 1990).

3 Matthew 14:28 and John 18:10.

4 Matthew 16:23.

5 Matthew 26:34-35, 69-74 (paraphrased).

6 Acts 1:15.

7 Acts 2:41 and Acts 4:4.

8 Ecclesiastes 2:26.

9 Chris Heath, "Family Secrets," *The Observer* (September 2, 2001).

10 Found at http://www.geocities.com/~spanoudi/topic-d2.html#despair.

11 Ecclesiastes 1:8

CHAPTER 3

4 J. Madison Davis, *The New York Times on The Sopranos* (New York: iBooks, 2000), pg. 39.

2 J. Madison Davis, *The New York Times on The Sopranos* (New York: iBooks, 2000), pg. 39.

3 The Message translation by Eugene Peterson (Colorado Springs: NavPress, 2002).

4 Matthew 5:45.

5 Annie Dillard, *Pilgrim at Tinker Creek* (New York: HarperPerennial, 1998), pg. 18.

6 Matthew 20:16.

7 Matthew 10:39.

8 Luke 12:15.

9 Luke 12:22-23.

10 Luke 14:12-14.

11 Sir Thomas Buxton, from E.M. Bounds, *Power Through Prayer*, (Minneapolis. World Wide Publications, 1989), ph 5

12 Hebrews 4:16.

13 C.S. Lewis, *Letters to Malcolm* (Fort Washington: Harvest Books,

1983), pg.22.

14 Psalm 41:4.

15 2 Chronicles 21:13.

16 Matthew 6:10.

17 James 4:2.

18 Psalm 40:12.

19 Found at

http://prayerfoundation.org/past_prayer_quotes_of_the_week_007.
htm

20 Found at http://www.gospelcom.net/cqod/cqod9810.htm

21 Oswald Chambers, *My Utmost for His Highest* (Grand Rapids:
Discovery House Publishers, 1994), October 17.

22 1 Corinthians 8:1.

CHAPTER 4

5 Augustus Y. Napier, *The Fragile Bond* (New York: HarperCollins, 1990),
ch. 13.

2 1 Peter 4:8.

3 Proverbs 13:24.

4 Proverbs 13:24.

5 Proverbs 22:6.

CHAPTER 5

6 1 Timothy 6:10.

2 Found in an article by Elesha Coffman, "The Root of All Kinds of
Evil," *Christianity Today* (Spring 2001), pg. 28.

3 Found in an article by Elesha Coffman, "The Root of All Kinds of
Evil," *Christianity Today* (Spring 2001), pg. 28.

4 Found in an article by Elesha Coffman, "The Root of All Kinds of
Evil," *Christianity Today* (Spring 2001), pg. 28.

5 Romans 7:19.

6 Luke 12:15.

7 Found in an article by Rodney Clapp, "Why the Devil takes VISA,"
Christianity Today (Oct. 7, 1996), pg. 18.

8 Found in an article by Elesha Coffman, "The Root of All Kinds of Evil," *Christianity Today* (Spring 2001), pg. 28.

9 Found in an article by Elesha Coffman, "The Root of All Kinds of Evil," *Christianity Today* (Spring 2001), pg. 28.

10 Beijing United Nations Women's Conference (1995).

11 Ecclesiastes 5:10.

12 Erich Fromm, *Escape from Freedom* (New York: Henry Holt, 1995), ch. 4.

13 Matthew 6:19-20.

CHAPTER 6

7 Matthew 7:7, KJV.

2 Malachi 3:6.

3 James 1:17.

4 St. Alphonsus Liguori, "A Good Confession," in an anthology entitled *To Any Christian*, pg. 192.

5 Matthew 10:26.

6 1 John 4:18.

7 James 5:16.

8 Dietrich Bonhoeffer, *Life Together* (New York: HarperSanFrancisco, 1978), pg. 116.

9 Thomas Keating, *The Human Condition* (Mahwah: Paulist Press, 1999), pg.17.

10 1 John 1:9.

11 C.S. Lewis, *The Problem of Pain* (New York: HarperSanFrancisco, 2001), pg.128.

12 David Hume, "Of the Immortality of the Soul," unpublished essay I, p. 594.

13 Romans 3:23

14 Terry Teachout, "The Family That Prays Together," *Crisis* (May 2000)

15 Mark 9:24.

16 T.S. (Thomas Stearns) Eliot, *The Cocktail Party* (New York: Harcourt, Brace and Co., 1950), act 1, sc. 3.

NOTES

CHAPTER 7

8 Nancy Friday, found at http://wisdom_quotes.tripod.com/mother-hood.html.

2 Genesis 2:18.

CHAPTER 8

9 Chris Heath, *The Observer*, found at
http://www.observer.co.uk/life/story/0,6903,545378,00.html.

2 Blaise Pascal, from Peter Kreeft's *Christianity for Modern Pagans* (Ft. Collins: Ignatius Press, 1993), pg. 213.

3 Thomas Keating, *The Human Condition* (Mahwah: Paulist Press) pg.7.

4 C. S. Lewis, *The Abolition of Man* (England: MacMillan Publishing, 1980) pg. 70.

5 John Rafferty, "Tony, Carmela, and God," PIQUE: Newsletter of the Secular Humanist Society of New York (June 2001).

6 John Piper, "The Fierce Fruit of Self-control," http://www.desiring-god.org/Online_Library/OnlineArticles/FreshWords/2001/051501. htm.

7 Genesis 3:5.

CHAPTER 9

10 J. Madison Davis, *The New York Times on The Sopranos* (New York: iBooks, 2000), pg. 81.

2 Matthew 5:39; John 13:34.

3 Acts 1:8.

CHAPTER 10

11 C.S. Lewis, *Mere Christianity* (New York: HarperSanFrancisco, 2001), pg. 117.

2 James 1:14-15

3 Al Capone, in an interview on October 17, 1931. *The Norton Book of Interviews*, edited by Christopher Silvester. Originally published in *The Penguin Book of Interviews*, NY

4 Isaiah 24:16

5 Joshua 1:5

6 2 Timothy 2:13

7 Luke 21:16

8 Isaiah 5:25; 9:12; 10:4; and others.

9 David Powlison, *The Journal of Biblical Counseling*, Volume 16, Number 1, Fall 1997, p. 39.

10 Psalm 4:4.

11 Proverbs 4:23.

12 Ephesians 4:31.

13 Ephesians 4:32.

CHAPTER 11

12 Author's interpretation of Ecclesiastes 3:1-8.

2 Ecclesiastes 2:18-19.

3 Ecclesiastes 2:23.

4 Blaise Pascal, Pensee #70, in Peter Kreeft's *Christianity for Modern Pagans* (Ft. Collins: Ignatius Press, 1993), p. 169.

5 Peter Kreeft, *Christianity For Modern Pagans* (Ignatius Press, 1993), pg. 169.

6 C.S. Lewis, *Letters of C.S. Lewis* (Fort Washington: Harvest Books, 1994), pg.285.

7 Matthew 7:7, KJV.

8 Blaise Pascal, from Peter Kreeft's *Christianity for Modern Pagans* (Ft. Collins: Ignatius Press, 1993) pg. 187.

9 Democritus, found at http://www.freedomsnest.com/cgi-bin/q.cgi?subject=pleasure.

10 Found at http://www.epicurus.net/menoeceus.html

11 Ecclesiastes 2:1-2.

12 Tim Jackson and Paul Carnes, *Designed for Desire*, (published electronically).

13 Harry Schaumburg, *False Intimacy* (Colorado Springs: Navpress, 1997)

14 Romans 1:22-24.

NOTES

CHAPTER 12

13 Genesis 2:25.

2 Song of Solomon 4:16.

3 John Eldredge, *Wild at Heart* (Nashville: Thomas Nelson, 2001) pg. 22.

4 Psalm 62:11-12.

5 Matthew 5:5.

6 Matthew 5:7.

7 C.S. Lewis, *God in the Dock* (Collins, 1979), pg. 321.

9 Chris Heath, "Family Secrets," *The Observer* (September 2, 2001).

CHAPTER 13

14 Colossians 1:16-18

2 Matthew 6:27.

3 Psalm 115:3.

4 Job 42:2.

5 Isaiah 46:11.

CONCLUSION

15 Matthew 7:7